5WS
6/7∂

Victory Through Vegetables

Joan Wiener

❧ Victory Through Vegetables

With a section of recipes from the Macrobiotic Diet by Barbara Thralls

Holt, Rinehart and Winston

New York   Chicago   San Francisco

Published simultaneously in Canada by Holt, Rinehart
and Winston of Canada, Limited.

Library of Congress Catalog Card Number: 78–122923

First Edition

Designer: Akinori

SBN: 03–085085–1 (Hardbound)
SBN: 03–085086–x (Paperback)

Printed in the United States of America

How I see things—am now—the way I'm going home is all my guru: SWAMI SATCHIDANANDA.

And the vibrations of—

Richie, my Rama and
  Al
Alan
Alison and Peter and
  Johnny
Ananda
Anasha
Annie and Michael
Anton, Francoise, Boris and
  Igor
Avalon
Barry and his Woodstock
  house
Ben and Kelly
The Bhagavad Gita
Bob
Bomber and Leslie
Booker and Ellen and their
  magic
Buffalo Springfield
Charlotte and her tarot deck
Crosby, Stills, Nash, Young
Daddy and Moth
Devi
Easy Rider
The Electric Lotus
Ellen

5A
Four days in White Lake
Gail and Burt
Gita and Ram Louise
Harvey and Bobbi
The Hog Farm
How to Know God
The I Ching
Jackie and Barry
Krishna
Mahesh and Parvathi
Malcolm and Alex
Marsha and Ma
Music from Big Pink
Nancy and Kala
Nashville Skyline
NineteenSixtySeven
Oscar
Ourika and Anne Colette
Peter and Steve
The Pt. Jervis House
Ramdas
Scott and Carol and Jeffrey
Sharon
Shree and Vij
Sub

Victory Through Vegetables contains:

**Part Two RECIPES FROM THE
MACROBIOTIC DIET**
BY BARBARA THRALLS

"But one thing is certain: the mighty river is rushing towards the ocean, and all the drops that constitute the stream will in time be drawn into that boundless ocean. So, in this life, with all its miseries and sorrows, its joys and smiles and tears, one thing is certain: that all things are rushing towards their goal and it is only a question of time when you and I, plants and animals, and every particle of life that exists, must reach the infinite Ocean of Perfection, must attain to Freedom, to God."

Swami Vivekananda

Part One

Recipes for Vegetarian Cooking

Revolution

We are part of nature.

Nature lives to serve.

The apple lives to be eaten, the candle to give light.

Does the apple eat of itself? The candle read by its own light?

They need never be taught how or why to give; that knowledge is in their cells. They do what is natural and what is natural is cosmic harmony, being in tune with the Universe.

Giving is harmony. It brings unity.

To give, the body and mind must be energized and that energy must be controlled and directed in order to purify the physical and mental processes. All through time, the enlightened have pointed out paths and disciplines to help in attaining energy and control—Yoga, Zen, Sufiism, Hasidism, the way of Christ. Choose the path that feels right. It must feel right if it is to help you.

The food you eat can be a tool or a great hindrance on your path. It is as important as your thoughts, the people you deal with, what you read. If your body is sick, your mind cannot focus properly. The gross portion of your food constitutes your body—but the subtle portion makes up the mind.

3

Of all foods, vegetables, fruits and grains are the easiest for the body to assimilate and transform into energy. The less packaged, preserved, and plastic food you put into your body, the fewer toxins the body has to eliminate, the more energy is at your command.

This too is revolution—purifying, redirecting energy, changing the body and mind, making the spirit more apparent, reaching freedom and peace. Only this revolution happens inside and the changes are permanent.

All the peace petitioned, paraded for is right where we are. Inside we are actually free and at peace.

All nature is helping us evolve, spurring our inner revolution. The whole Universe is our guru.

And each time we smile, each time we choose love over anger, each time we hold out our hands to each other, incredible battles are won, amazing barriers are torn down. The cheers are all silence. The battle cry is OM. Each victory brings us closer to home.

Hints

Everybody I've lived with and been with has put themselves into this book—and while some of these recipes are quite basic or steady, none of them is dull. Like these people, they are all alive and can help you grow. Organize your kitchen as a Zen artist organizes his studio. As he works his brushes beforehand, and his inks, you should lay out your utensils and ingredients step by step before proceeding with a recipe. Perform the act of cooking in a relaxed way and transfer that calm and love into your foods. If preparation becomes a furied race around the kitchen, your meal will be infused with that type of frantic vibration. Go easy.

When, through my yoga practice, my husband and I first became vegetarians, we were the only ones among a rather large group of people, and the kitchen at that time was my thing. Now, with an increasing flow of my friends interested in eating vegetables— either for spiritual ideals or for reasons of health (low cholesterol, high vitamin and protein content) or money (low cost)—I have had to give up my attachment to the kitchen through the encumbrance of my brothers and sisters. In cases such as this, choose a leader before preparing a meal. If you cook with other people, each person should have a task that doesn't infringe on his neighbor.

Many of the recipes in this book require only a short cooking time. A list of these simple recipes can be found on p. 149.

The ingredients listed are rarely exotic and should be obtainable locally, rounded up in one major shopping trip. Vegetables and fruits should be gotten as fresh as possible.

If you are into it, change any of the recipes as you like, adding or subtracting ingredients. Be daring.

The ingredients have been listed in order categorically. On the left side are vegetables and fruits (fresh and dried), flour and grains. On the right are juices, spices, bottled goods and dry goods. This has been done mainly for shopping convenience. If you have to do last minute buying, it is easier to find what you'll need.

Read the measured amount of a particular ingredient in this way:

½ c. almonds, blanched and chopped means you should have ½ cup of almonds after blanching and chopping.

Abbreviations:

> c. = cup
> tsp. = teaspoon
> tbsp. = tablespoon
> mins. = minutes
> hr. = hour(s)
> med. = medium

Each recipe has been figured for four unless otherwise noted.

And, with any food you choose to eat, chew it well,

liquefy your solids through chewing rather than washing down hunks of food with liquids.

Part Two is a very beautiful section on macrobiotics written by my friend Barbara, although she doesn't advocate eating macrobiotic foods exclusively. Her quantity abbreviations are the same as mine plus qt. = quart and her section has its own introduction, food lists, and so on.

Staples

Staple foods (as opposed to the fresh foods you buy daily or weekly) should be well labeled and stored in sealed, transparent containers.

SPICES, DRIED HERBS, SALTS, ETC.

Allspice	Garlic powder
Anise seed	Ginger
Basil	Ground mustard
Bay leaves	Mace
Black pepper	Marjoram
Cardamon powder	Mustard seeds
Cayenne pepper	Nutmeg
Celery salt	Onion powder
Chili powder	Paprika
Chives	Parsley flakes
Cinnamon	Sage
Cloves	Salt (regular)
Coriander	Sea salt
Cumin	Sesame salt
Curry powder	Thyme
Dill weed	Turmeric

FLOUR

Rye	Unbleached white
Soy	Whole wheat

GRAINS AND CEREALS

Brown rice	Pearl barley
Bulgur wheat	Raw (white) rice
Cornmeal	Rolled oats
Couscous	Semolina
Farina	Soy grits

Wheat germ

PEAS AND BEANS

Black beans	Kidney beans
Chickpeas	Lentils

Soybeans

DRIED FRUITS, NUTS AND SEEDS

Dates	Pecans or walnuts
Raisins	(unsalted)
Almonds (unsalted)	Pine nuts (pignolias)
Cashews (unsalted)	Caraway seeds
Peanuts (raw)	Sesame seeds

Sunflower seeds

BOTTLED GOODS

Almond extract	Oil (corn or peanut)
Honey	Oil (olive)
Lemon juice	Relish (pickle)
Lime juice	Soy sauce
Maple syrup	Vanilla extract
Molasses	Vinegar

DRY GOODS

Baking powder
Baking soda
Brown sugar
Cornstarch or
    arrowroot

Raw sugar
Vegetable bouillon
cubes
Yeast

Tools

The proper cooking tools, kept in good repair and set up in an orderly fashion are a necessity to hassle-free cooking.

Have your old man sharpen your knives every now and again as fresh vegetables are difficult to cut through with dull equipment.

Cast-iron pots and pans are a groove to work with, but certain things should be known about them. Never soak them in water as they tend to rust. Instead, rinse them out with a little detergent and dry them immediately over a low flame, rather than with a towel. If they do rust (somebody thought they would surprise you by doing the dishes), rub them with a bit of oil and dry them over a low flame.

Save your money and get a blender. They are just great for making fresh vegetable or fruit drinks, dressings, desserts, and so on. If you are into camping or live without electricity, a hand grinder is almost as handy as a blender.

Following is a list of utensils helpful in vegetarian cookery.

Blender or grinder
Baking pans (two)
Chopper
Colander
Cookie sheets (two)
Cutting board
Deep-frying pan
Frying pan (small)
Frying pan (medium)
Frying pan (large)
Glass jars (various sizes)
Grater
Griddle
Knives (various sizes)
Ladle
Loaf pans (three)
Masher
Measuring cups (two)
Measuring spoons (1 set)

Mixing bowl (small)
Mixing bowl (medium)
Mixing bowl (large)
Paper towels
Pastry brush
Peeler
Pie plates (two)
Pot (large)
Pots (two, medium)
Rolling pin
Saucepan (small)
Saucepan (medium)
Saucepan (large)
Spatula
Strainer
Wire whip
Wooden spoons (two)

Optional: Chinese wok (frying pan)

Increase the amount of your tools geometrically for the number of cooks and people living in your house.

Recipes

🪷 BASIC INGREDIENTS

Of the following basics, ghee, soybean milk, bean curd, and yoghurt should be kept well sealed and refrigerated. When I prepare these foods, I usually make enough to last a week or two. Keeping them any longer may mean spoilage.

PASTA

2 c. whole wheat	1 tsp. salt
or unbleached white	⅔ c. water
flour	
Flour for rolling	

In bowl, combine ingredients. Knead for about 5 mins. Let stand, covered, ½ hr.

Flour board or tabletop and roll out mixture until thin. Cut to desired shape (thin noodles, lasagna noodles, etc.).

For plain pasta, boil in water for 30 to 45 mins.

Note: The bleached white noodles one comes upon in the local supermarkets are, for the most part, nowhere. Though rolling your own takes longer, the end product will give you more energy.

BEANS

Beans can supply all the protein your system needs for an indefinite time. Soybeans, especially, provide twice as much protein as meat or fish and three times as much as eggs. There is a time element involved, however, in the preparation of dried beans.

First, they should be soaked overnight. If you intend to soak them longer (suppose you are leaving the house for a couple of days), refrigerate them to prevent fermentation. After soaking, the beans should be cooked in boiling water until tender (4 to 5 hrs.), adding more water if necessary as it is absorbed. Then the beans should stand for 1 or 2 hrs. so that the gaseous elements are released.

GHEE

1 lb. butter

In saucepan, over medium flame, heat the butter until a foam rises to the top of the pan. Skim off this foam (the solids) and discard or preserve for frying foods. Continue this heating and skimming process until the liquid in the pan is a clear yellow. Store this ghee in a clean glass jar, covered well (1 lb. of butter will make about ½ lb. ghee).

Ghee is best used in the preparation of Indian foods but tastes out of sight on toast or crackers.

SOYBEAN MILK AND SOY CHAFF

1 c. soybeans   Water for soaking
                       6 c. water

In bowl, soak beans overnight in enough water to cover. Grind through chopper or chop in blender. In pot, boil beans in 6 c. water for 5 mins. Lower flame and simmer beans for 15 mins. in covered pot. Drain chaff in strainer. The liquid is also called soybean milk.

If you are using a recipe that calls for soy milk or chaff, prepare the ingredients beforehand for the sake of convenience.

BEAN CURD

In bowl or pan, let soybean milk stand in a warm place till it thickens. When this happens, separate thick part from surrounding water.

Put this thick part (the curd) in enough water to cover and boil for 5 mins.

Remove. Drain. Use in recipes which call for chicken as, combined with other ingredients, it has an almost chicken-like taste. Plain, however, it is practically tasteless and can be used with almost anything.

Bean curd (also called Tofu or soy cheese) can be obtained commercially, usually at Oriental food stores. It comes in cans or is made daily in squares.

INSTANT BEAN CURD

Add 2 tbsp. lemon juice to boiled soy milk, stirring.
Let milk cool and congeal. Drain curds.

YOGHURT

1 quart milk
1 tbsp. plain yoghurt
   (commercial or
   homemade)

In saucepan, boil milk and let stand until lukewarm.
   Spoon yoghurt into clean glass jar and pour lukewarm milk over it. Cover jar tightly.
   Fill a large pot with hot water (enough to completely surround jar while upright). Let jar stand in
this water, covered. When water cools, refill pot with
fresh warm water. In about 5 hrs. the milk and yoghurt
starter will have formed fresh yoghurt.
   Always save a tbsp. of yoghurt to use as a starter
for the next batch.

🌿 BEVERAGES

*If you have a blender or shaker, you can easily sup-
plement the following drinks with your own vegetable
and fruit combinations.*

BANANA-NUT WHIP

1 c. milk or skimmed
  milk
½ c. almonds, blanched
½ c. unsalted peanuts,
  blanched
½ banana, peeled and
  sliced

2½ tbsp. molasses

Liquefy in blender.
Serves 2.

LASEY

2 tbsp. plain yoghurt

8 oz. glass of water
¼ tsp. lemon juice
Dash of salt
Dash of pepper
Dash of coriander

Combine ingredients and add ice cubes.
Serves 1.

LIQUID RASPBERRY TART

¼ c. raspberries
  (frozen or fresh. If
  fresh, add 1 tbsp.
  honey)
2 tbsp. raisins

2 c. apple juice
1 tbsp. lime juice

Combine ingredients in blender at high speed.

STRAWBERRY SHERBET DRINK

1 package frozen straw- ½ c. water
berries ½ tsp. almond extract
¾ c. milk

Combine ingredients in blender at high speed.

🪷 BREAD

Bread baking should be given time and patience. In the case of yeast breads, consider, before embarking on that project, the time your dough will take to rise. If the dough doesn't rise enough, or if it rises too much, the taste of the bread will lose out.

When melting the yeast, your water should always be lukewarm. Water that is too hot or too cold will kill off the yeast.

APPLECREAM BISCUITS

2 c. whole wheat flour   1 tbsp. baking powder
1 c. unbleached white   ¼ tsp. baking soda
flour   1 tsp. salt
¼ c. milk   1 tsp. cinnamon
½ c. yoghurt   2 tbsp. brown sugar
½ c. sour cream   Oil for cookie sheets
¼ c. shelled sunflower
seeds, chopped
2 med. apples, peeled
and grated

In bowl, blend flours, baking powder, baking soda, and salt. Mix in all other ingredients. Knead on well-floured board or table until a soft, smooth dough is formed. Add more flour, if necessary, to gain this consistency.

With rolling pin, roll dough out to a ½-inch thickness.

Preheat oven to 400°.

Cut dough in circles, using the top of a large-rimmed glass. Bake for 15 to 20 mins. on cookie sheets.

CARAWAY RYE

2 c. rye flour	1 cake or 1 package
3 c. unbleached white	yeast
flour	1 c. lukewarm water
2 tbsp. caraway seeds	2 tbsp. honey
2 tbsp. sesame seeds	2 tsp. salt
Flour for kneading	2 tbsp. corn oil
	Oil for bowls and pans

In bowl, dissolve yeast in lukewarm water. In another bowl, combine flour, caraway and sesame seeds, honey, salt, and oil. Add yeast mixture.

Knead on well-floured board or tabletop, until a soft, smooth dough is formed. Add more flour, if necessary, to gain this consistency.

Form into a smooth ball. Place ball in oiled bowl. Oil top of ball.

Allow dough to double in a warm place, covered (about 1 hr.).

Shape dough into two loaves on oiled cookie sheet. Meanwhile preheat oven to 375°. Bake for 50 mins. or until center is firm.

CORN BREAD

1 c. cornmeal	1 cake or 1 package
½ c. uncooked corn	yeast
kernels	1 c. lukewarm water
4 c. whole wheat flour	¼ c. honey
2 c. unbleached white	¼ c. molasses
flour	2 tsp. salt
Flour for kneading	2 tbsp. corn oil
	2 c. hot water
	Oil for bowl and pan

In bowl, dissolve yeast in lukewarm water. In another bowl, combine corn kernels, cornmeal, honey, molasses, salt, and 2 tbsp. oil in hot water. When hot water has cooled, add yeast mixture. In a third bowl, combine whole wheat and unbleached flours. Add to other ingredients by the cup.

Knead on well-floured board or tabletop, until a soft, smooth dough is formed. Add more flour, if necessary, to gain this consistency.

Form into a smooth ball. Place ball in oiled bowl. Oil top of ball.

Allow dough to double in a warm place, covered (about 1 hr.). Then punch dough down (press air out).

Separate dough into two oiled loaf pans. Allow dough to rise in pans in a warm place, covered by a towel (about 1 hr.).

Preheat oven to 400°. Bake for 50 mins. or until center is firm.

DOWN HOME CRUNCHY FIG BREAD

1 c. figs, chopped	1 c. hot orange or
½ tsp. finely grated	pineapple-grape-
orange peel	fruit juice
3 c. whole wheat flour	1 tsp. salt
½ c. filberts or hazel-	1 tbsp. baking powder
nuts, chopped	1 c. light or dark
2 tbsp. wheat germ	brown sugar
	¼ tsp. mace (the
	spice)
	¼ c. honey
	Oil for loaf pan

In bowl, soak figs in juice for 30 to 60 mins. In another bowl, mix together orange peel, flour, salt, baking powder, sugar, and mace. Add filberts, wheat germ, honey, and figs, mixing well to form a sticky, granular batter. Preheat oven to 350°. Pour batter into oiled loaf pan. Bake for 1¼ hrs.

HERB BREAD

2 c. scalded milk	1 cake or 1 package
2 c. unbleached white	yeast
flour	¼ c. lukewarm water
¼ c. soy flour	2 tbsp. oil
2 to 3 c. whole wheat	3 tbsp. honey
flour	1 tsp. sage
½ c. yellow or black	½ tsp. marjoram
raisins	1 tbsp. dill
Flour for kneading	1 tbsp. salt
	1 tsp. clove powder
	2 tbsp. melted butter
	Oil for bowl and pans

In bowl, dissolve yeast in lukewarm water.

In another bowl, combine milk, 2 tbsp. oil, honey, spices, salt, raisins, and butter.

In a third bowl, combine unbleached, soy, and whole wheat flours. Add to other ingredients a little at a time.

Knead on well-floured board or tabletop, until a soft, smooth dough is formed. Add more flour, if necessary, to gain this consistency.

Form into a smooth ball. Place ball in oiled bowl. Oil top of ball.

Allow dough to double in a warm place, covered (about 1 hr.). Punch dough down (press air out).

Separate dough into two loaf pans. Allow dough to rise again in pans in a warm place, covered by a towel (about 1 hr.).

Meanwhile preheat oven to 400°. Bake loaves for 50 mins. or until center is firm.

INCREDIBLE WHOLE WHEAT
BREAD PARVATHI

9 c. whole wheat flour	3 c. hot water
1 c. oat or soy flour	3 tbsp. packaged yeast
	1 c. honey
	1 tbsp. salt
	¼ c. corn oil
	Oil for bowls
	Melted butter for
	bread pans

In large mixing bowl, dissolve honey in hot water. Cool to a temperature of approximately 100 degrees and then add yeast.

Let yeast stand until soft (about 5 mins.) Add salt,

corn oil, and 6 c. whole wheat flour. Mix well. Beat for 100 strokes.

Add 2 c. whole wheat flour and oat or soy flour. Dust board or tabletop with 1 c. whole wheat flour. With rolling pin, roll out bread dough. Knead dough. Leave one side of dough always on the bottom during kneading so that it remains flat.

Oil large bowl or pot and place dough in smooth side up. Oil top.

Let dough stand in warm place until doubled (about 1 hr.). Punch down, squeezing air out of dough, and let stand until doubled again.

With melted butter, grease 3 small or 2 regular-size bread pans. Punch dough down. Shape into 2 or 3 loaves. Place loaves in pans, smooth side up. Let stand for ½ hr., or until batter rises to top of pans. Meanwhile preheat oven to 350°. Bake for 50 mins. for 3 loaves; 70 mins. for 2 loaves.

Love and patience are necessary for really groovy bread so allow yourself plenty of time to make it.

MOLASSES BREAD

1¼ c. whole wheat flour	1 tsp. baking powder 1 tsp. baking soda
1¼ c. unbleached white flour	1 tsp. salt 4 tbsp. butter, melted
¼ c. raisins	1 tsp. vinegar
1½ c. milk	¼ c. molasses
	¼ c. honey
	Melted butter for bread pan

In large bowl, combine flours, baking powder, baking soda, salt, and butter. In cup, add vinegar to milk, forming sour milk. Add to flour mixture. Mix in raisins, molasses, and honey. Brush melted butter all over inside of bread pan. Let batter stand for 20 mins. Preheat oven to 375°. Spoon batter into pan. Bake for 50 mins.

THREE INDIAN BREADS

The dough used for all three breads is the same. The difference occurs in the shaping of the dough and in its cooking.

Dough:

1 c. unbleached white flour	**1 tsp. salt**
	2 tbsp. melted ghee
1 c. whole wheat flour	**½ to ¾ c. water**

Combine flours and salt. Stir in ghee.
  Slowly add the water, using as much as necessary to get a dough that is not actually soft but that is elastic.
  Allow dough to stand for ½ hr.

CHAPATTI

Dough as above	**Ghee for griddle or frying pan**

On floured board or tabletop, shape dough into an oblong. Form medium-sized balls from the oblong. Flatten.

Heat griddle or frying pan. Melt enough ghee to cover bottom with a film. With a spatula, place a chapatti on griddle or pan. Flip chapatti until brown spots form on both sides. Let cool.

POORI

Dough as above   Oil for deep frying

On floured board or tabletop, shape dough into an oblong. Form small balls from the oblong. Flatten. Heat oil in deep-frying pan, adjusting heat so that it is neither too hot nor too cool. If poori swells up immediately when put into the oil, it is a good temperature. Drain.

PARATHA

Dough as above   Ghee for parathas and
                              griddle or pan

On floured board or tabletop, shape dough into an oblong. Form medium-sized balls from the oblong.
Roll out into flat circles. Brush with ghee. Fold in half. Brush with ghee. Fold in half again. Brush with ghee. Roll this triangle into a circle.
Brush ghee on griddle or frying pan. Place paratha in pan. When paratha begins to puff up, turn. Turn twice. Each time paratha is turned, brush it with ghee.

BUTTER

These two basic recipes can be adapted to the making of any type of nut or fruit butter.

FILBERT BUTTER

1 c. filberts, chopped

A little less than 3 tbsp. peanut oil
4 tsp. honey

Combine ingredients in blender at medium to high speed.

Note: Cashews or any other oily nut can be substituted for filberts.

PLUM BUTTER

2 plums, chopped

2 tbsp. honey
1 tbsp. molasses
½ c. butter
1 tsp. nutmeg

Combine ingredients in blender at medium to high speed.

🌼 SOUP

Every member of my household got into the soup—
Harvey demoniacally adding zip to it, Richie asking if
it was good as Campbell's, Bobby leafing through notes.
All of these soups are filling enough to make a meal
in themselves.

ALEX'S RESIDENCE CHEESE AND POTATO SOUP

1 med. onion, sliced
2 c. potatoes, peeled and diced
1 carrot, peeled and sliced
1 parsnip, peeled and sliced
2 stalks celery, sliced
3 pieces pumpernickel or rye bread, crusts removed and diced
½ c. American cheese, chopped

2 tbsp. butter
6 cups water
½ tsp. pepper
1 tsp. salt
1 tbsp. fresh parsley, chopped

In pot, sauté onion in butter for 3 mins. Add all other ingredients. Cover. Simmer for 1 hr.

APPLE SPICE SOUP

2½ large Rome apples, peeled and sliced	5 c. water
3 slices whole wheat bread, cut in chunks	½ tsp. nutmeg
	1 tsp. cinnamon
	¼ tsp. powdered cloves
⅔ c. black or yellow raisins	3 tbsp. honey
1 tbsp. sour cream	

In pot, combine water, apples, raisins, spices, honey. When water boils, add bread. Cover. Simmer over low flame for 1 hr.
Add sour cream, stirring. Cook for 5 mins. more.

ASIAN VEGETABLE SOUP

¼ c. scallions, chopped	1 tbsp. corn or peanut oil
1 c. celery, sliced	1 vegetable bouillon cube
½ c. mushrooms, sliced	2 tsp. cornstarch or 1 tsp. arrowroot
¼ c. bean sprouts	
1 c. lettuce, sliced	6 c. warm water
1½ c. carrots, sliced	1 tbsp. soy sauce
⅓ c. peas	

In pot, sauté scallions in oil for 3 mins.
In cup, dissolve bouillon cube and cornstarch in water. Add soy sauce. Pour into pot.
Add all other ingredients. Cover. Cook over low flame for 20 to 30 mins.

BEET AND PEA SOUP

8 med. beets, grated	8 c. water
½ c. split peas	2 tbsp. honey
½ c. scallions, chopped	1 tbsp. salt
¼ c. sour cream	½ tbsp. dill weed

In pot, combine beets, split peas, scallions, honey, and water. Cover. Cook over low flame for 1 hr. Add salt and dill weed. Cook for 10 mins. Add sour cream just before serving. Serve hot or cold.

CELERY-CHEESE SOUP

1 c. celery, minced	1½ tbsp. corn or pea-
½ c. onion, minced	nut oil
⅔ c. green pepper, diced	1½ tbsp. salt
	¼ tsp. basil
1 c. sour cream	¼ tsp. thyme
2 c. cottage cheese	3 c. water
1 c. milk	

In pot, sauté celery, onions, and pepper in oil for 10 mins.
Add salt, basil, thyme, water, and milk. Cook over low flame, covered, for ½ hr.
Add sour cream and cottage cheese, cook for 5 mins. longer.

CELERY-CREAM SOUP

4 heaping tbsp. whole wheat flour	4 tbsp. butter
2½ c. celery with tops, diced	2½ c. water
	½ tsp. celery salt
¾ c. carrots, diced	½ tsp. marjoram
2 c. milk or light cream	2 tsp. salt
½ c. yoghurt or sour cream	

In pot, melt butter. Briskly stir in flour, with a fork, to
form a paste. Slowly add water, stirring.
Add vegetables, salts, and marjoram. Cover and
simmer for 35 mins.
Add milk or cream, cover, simmer for 10 mins.
Add yoghurt or sour cream and serve.

COMBI-BEAN SOUP

½ med. onion, chopped	1 clove garlic, minced
1 c. chick-peas, cooked	1 tbsp. butter
½ c. kidney beans, cooked	1½ tbsp. salt
2 c. cabbage, chopped	1 tsp. pepper
1 c. carrots, diced	6 c. water
1 c. c. celery, diced	
2 c. potatoes, peeled and diced	
2 tbsp. Parmesan cheese, grated	

In large pot, sauté onions and garlic in butter until onions are yellow.

Add all other ingredients. Cook, covered, over low flame for at least 1 hr.; 2 or 3 hrs. would be even better.

CREAM OF RICE AND SOYBEAN SOUP

1 c. soybeans, cooked	1 c. water
1 c. brown rice, cooked	2 tbsp. sesame salt
¼ c. almonds, halved	(ground sesame
lengthwise	seeds and sea salt)
2 c. milk	1 tsp. nutmeg

In pot, combine ingredients. Heat for 10 mins.

Note: If you do not eat this soup as soon as it is heated, chances are the rice and soybeans will absorb all the liquid.

CREAM OF PEA SOUP IN A FLASH

2 packages frozen peas	1 c. water
2 tbsp. sour cream	
1 c. milk	

In saucepan, thaw peas as per directions on package. Drain.

In blender, at high speed, combine peas, 1 c. of water, milk, and sour cream. Serve hot or cold.

FRUIT SOUP

3 plums, pitted and sliced	6 c. warm water
2 med. peaches, pitted and sliced	1 tbsp. cornstarch or ½ tbsp. arrowroot
2 tbsp. cottage cheese	4 tbsp. honey
½ tbsp. sour cream	2 tsp. cinnamon

In pot, dissolve cornstarch in water, stirring so lumps do not form. Add fruit, honey, and cinnamon to pot. Cover. Simmer for 1 hr.

Add cottage cheese (do not allow cottage cheese to boil or it will harden) and sour cream and serve.

HARVEY'S SESAME SPINACH SOUP

6 c. spinach, steamed and chopped	2 tbsp. peanut oil
2 tbsp. sesame seeds	1 tbsp. ginger, powdered
	5 tbsp. soy sauce
	¼ tsp. pepper
	3 tsp. cornstarch or 2 tsp. arrowroot
	1 vegetable bouillon cube
	5 c. warm water

In large pot, sauté ginger and sesame seeds in oil for 3 mins.

Mix cornstarch and bouillon cube in 5 c. water, making sure both are dissolved.

Add water and other ingredients to pot. Cook over low flame for 30 to 45 mins.

HOT GAZPACHO

3 med. tomatoes
1½ green peppers,
    cored and sliced
2 carrots, peeled and
    sliced
1 cucumber, peeled
    and sliced

1 c. warm water
1 tsp. garlic
½ tsp. black pepper
½ tsp. parsley flakes
¼ tsp. basil
¼ tsp. thyme
1 tsp. onion powder
½ tsp. salt
1 tsp. lemon juice

In pot, parboil tomatoes for 5 mins. Peel. Combine all ingredients in blender or run through grinder. Can also be served cold by chilling for 1 hr.

INDIAN LENTIL SOUP (Dal)

1 c. lentils, washed
1 med. onion, chopped

7 c. water
2 tbsp. corn or pea-
    nut oil
1 tbsp. salt
¼ tsp. chili powder
1 tsp. turmeric
½ tsp. cumin seeds
1 tsp. ground
    coriander
2 tbsp. butter

In pot, cook lentils in water until tender (1 to 2 hrs.). Mash lentils without draining.

In frying pan, sauté onions in oil until yellow. Add salt and spices to onion and sauté for 1 min.

Add onions, spices, and butter to lentils. Cook for ½ hr. longer. Add a little more salt if necessary.

MUSHROOM-BARLEY SOUP

2 c. mushrooms, sliced	2 tbsp. butter
1 large onion, sliced	8 c. water
1 c. pearl barley	¼ tsp. pepper
1 c. milk	1 tbsp. salt
	2 bay leaves

In pot, sauté mushrooms and onion in butter for 5 mins. Add water. Bring to boil. Add barley, pepper, salt, and bay leaves. Cover. Cook over low heat for 1 hr. or until barley is soft. Add milk. Cook for 5 mins. longer.

NOODLE-BEAN SOUP

½ c. kidney beans, cooked	1 vegetable bouillon cube
½ c. black beans, cooked or 1 c. kidney beans, cooked	6 c. warm water
	1 tbsp. vinegar
1 c. turnips, diced	2 tbsp. soy sauce
1 c. lettuce, chopped	2 tsp. salt
2 scallions, chopped	¼ tsp. chili powder
2½ c. noodles, uncooked	¼ tsp. black pepper
2 tbsp. sesame seeds	

In pot, dissolve bouillon cube in water. Add all other ingredients. Cover and cook over low flame for 20 to 30 mins.

PINAPOTATO SOUP

4 large sweet potatoes	4 c. water
1 med. onion, sliced	1 tbsp. mustard seeds
1 c. carrots, diced	3 tbsp. butter
1 c. tomatoes, diced	1 tsp. salt
½ c. crushed pineapple, drained	
1 c. milk	

In pot, boil potatoes in water until soft. Remove from water, peel, and mash.

In frying pan, sauté onions in 2 tbsp. butter until yellow. Add mustard seeds and heat until they begin to pop.

Combine potatoes and onion mixture and return to the cooking water.

Add all other ingredients. Cook, covered, over low flame for ½ hr.

THICKEST CABBAGE SOUP

7 c. cabbage, chopped	3 tbsp. corn or peanut oil
1 small onion, chopped	1 tbsp. butter
1 c. tomatoes, diced	4½ c. water
2 pieces whole wheat or rye bread, diced	1 tbsp. salt
1 tbsp. sesame seeds	2 tbsp. soy sauce
	⅛ tsp. cayenne pepper

In large pot, sauté cabbage, onion, and sesame seeds in oil over low flame for 10 mins.

Stir in other ingredients. Cook, covered, over medium flame for 1 to 2 hrs.

TOMATO BISQUE

6 c. tomatoes, parboiled (boil in water for 5 mins.), peeled and diced	2 c. water
	2 tbsp. salt
	½ tsp. dill
	½ tsp. cloves, ground
⅔ c. onions, minced	1 tsp. raw sugar
½ tsp. sesame seeds	1 tbsp. butter
2 c. milk	

In large pot, place vegetables, water, salt, dill, cloves, seeds, and sugar. Heat over medium flame for ½ hr.

Add butter and milk, stirring as you add. Let soup simmer for 15 mins. more.

❈ COLD DISHES

Included in this section are cereals, salads, and spreads.

The two cereals are particularly groovy for lunch if you need a lot of energy to carry you through the rest of the day.

Salads and spreads are really nice for dinner because these foods are easily digested before you go to bed, resulting in deeper, more restful sleep.

CEREALS

BOBBY'S CEREAL THING

½ c. corn or frosted   ¼ c. raw sugar
   flakes
½ c. uncooked rolled
   oats
⅓ c. soy grits
½ c. raisins
⅓ c. almonds, chopped
⅓ c. grated coconut
2 med. apples, chopped
Milk to taste

Combine all ingredients except milk.
Serve with milk.
It can also be made in quantity and stored in a closed container, but do not include the apples as they will spoil. Add them just before eating.

VEGIE-SPEED

½ c. uncooked rolled
   oats
½ banana, sliced
1 tbsp. sesame seeds
2 tbsp. raisins
¼ c. almonds, cut in
   half

¼ c. cashews, cut in
   half

Mix ingredients together and eat with or without milk.
It is out of sight for getting energy.
Serves 1.

SALADS

BAMBU SALAD

1 c. bamboo shoots
1 c. bean sprouts
½ c. water chestnuts,
   chopped
½ c. celery, diced
¾ c. string beans,
   chopped
1 c. watercress,
   chopped
1 tbsp. sesame seeds

In bowl, combine ingredients.
Serve with or without a dressing.

COLE SLAW

4 c. cabbage,
   shredded
1½ c. carrots, grated
1½ c. parsnips, grated
½ c. sour cream

1 tsp. salt
1 tsp. dill weed
½ tsp. pepper

In bowl, combine ingredients well.

FALL SALAD

1 small Romaine let-
    tuce, torn in bite-
    size pieces
1 small Boston lettuce,
    chopped
1 med. tomato, cut into
    8 pieces
1 c. string beans, sliced
½ c. peas
½ c. radishes, sliced
1 avocado, cut in
    chunks
½ c. corn
¼ c. pine nuts
½ c. almonds, halved
1 pint cottage cheese,
    creamed type
1 c. Gouda or Bonbel
    cheese, cut in
    chunks

Toss ingredients together.

GITA'S LUNCH PAIL SPECIAL

Yesterday's leftover brown rice or other grain is a
good addition to a salad as follows:

2 c. brown rice or other
   grain, cooked
4 c. lettuce, chopped
2 c. tomatoes, diced
1 onion, chopped
2 green peppers,
   chopped
Any leftover vegetables

2 tsp. peanut oil
½ tsp. lemon juice

Combine ingredients.

HERBED CHICK-PEA SALAD

1 c. chick-peas, cooked,
   but firm
½ cucumber, sliced
¼ c. fresh mint,
   chopped
5 c. Chinese lettuce or
   iceberg lettuce,
   chopped and crispy
2 tbsp. shelled sun-
   flower seeds

1 tbsp. parsley flakes
2 tsp. dill

In bowl, combine ingredients.

MALAYSIA SALAD

3 c. Romaine lettuce,
chopped well
½ c. green pepper,
diced
¼ c. onions, diced
½ c. cucumber, diced
¼ c. water chestnuts,
diced
¼ c. bamboo shoots,
chopped
½ c. peanuts, cut in
half lengthwise

2 tbsp. lemon juice

Combine ingredients.

POTATO SALAD ROTTENBERG

2 large potatoes, peeled
and quartered
1 stalk celery, diced
1 small onion, minced
2 tbsp. sour cream

Water for boiling
½ tsp. salt
¼ tsp. pepper
¼ tsp. parsley flakes
1 tsp. vinegar
1 tbsp. pickle relish

In pot, boil potatoes for 15 mins. Drain. Cut in chunks.
In bowl, combine potato chunks with all other ingredients, tossing. Chill for at least ½ hr.

SOY NUT SALAD

1 c. soy nuts (please   ½ tsp. salt
   see p. 93)
1 c. Chinese lettuce,
   chopped
4 to 5 c. spinach,
   washed well and
   chopped

Toss ingredients together in salad bowl.

SUMMER SALAD

1 small lettuce, torn   1 tbsp. soy sauce
   into bite-size pieces
1 med. carrot, grated
   or sliced thin
1 apple, diced
1 pear, diced
1 banana, sliced in 1″
   pieces
1 green pepper, cored
   and diced
1 scallion, minced
1 tbsp. almonds, cut in
   half
1 tbsp. shelled sun-
   flower seeds
1 tbsp. sesame seeds
½ c. raisins
1 tbsp. wheat germ
2 tbsp. sour cream or
   plain yoghurt

In bowl, combine vegetables, fruit, nuts, seeds, and wheat germ. In cup, mix sour cream or yoghurt and soy sauce. Pour over salad mixture.

TART SALAD

3 med. large cucumbers, sliced fairly thin	¼ c. oil
	¼ c. vinegar
	2 tsp. salt
1½ c. radishes, sliced thin	1 tsp. parsley flakes
	1 tbsp. honey

In bowl, combine ingredients. Chill for at least ½ hr.

SPREADS

AVOCADO WHIP

1 avocado	½ tsp. salt
2 scallions, chopped	1 tsp. lime juice
¼ c. mixed nuts, chopped	

Combine ingredients in blender at medium or high speed.

CURD SANDWICH SPREAD

1 c. bean curd, mashed	1 tbsp. Bob's Mayo
¾ c. celery, minced	(please see p. 46)
½ c. green pepper, minced	Salt to taste

In bowl, mix ingredients.

EGGPLANT SPREAD
(*with a Little Zip to It*)

1 med. eggplant, diced	2 tbsp. olive or corn oil
1 med. onion, chopped	1 tsp. salt
3 tbsp. wheat germ	

In covered pan, sauté eggplant and onion in oil for 15 mins.

Spoon eggplant and onion into bowl. Mix with wheat germ and salt. Chop fine.

HEALTH SALAD SPREAD

2 c. lettuce, shredded
1 pear, grated
1 green pepper, grated
2 stalks celery, grated
2 tbsp. cottage cheese

In bowl, combine ingredients well.

MIMI ALTERMAN'S CARROT "SALMON"

6 carrots, chopped	2 tbsp. pickle relish
½ c. unsalted cashews, chopped	1½ tbsp. Bob's Mayo (please see p. 46)
½ c. peanuts, chopped	

Combine carrots and nuts in blender or put through grinder. In bowl, mix all ingredients together well.

MUSHROOM SPREAD

3 c. mushrooms, sliced	1 tbsp. corn or peanut oil
2 small onions, sliced	1 tbsp. butter
1½ tsp. sour cream	Salt to taste

In pan, sauté mushrooms and onions in oil and butter until mushrooms are brown and onions transparent. Spoon into wooden bowl and chop well. Stir in sour cream and salt.

SHREE'S SAN FRANCISCO GUACAMOLE

1 avocado, peeled and sliced	1½ tbsp. lemon juice
	½ tsp. salt
½ onion, chopped	1 tsp. chili powder
½ tomato, chopped	¼ tsp. pepper

Combine all ingredients in blender or run through grinder.

Note: The above makes enough guacamole for use as a spread. To use as a main course, double the amount.

🌺 DRESSINGS AND SAUCES

Use the dressings for salads and spreads, the sauces with such main courses as loaves.

DRESSINGS

BOB'S MAYO

2 tbsp. soy flour

4 tbsp. water
½ c. oil
1 tsp. salt
Dash lemon juice

In saucepan, boil flour and water. Rapidly stir in oil, salt, and lemon juice.

RUSSIAN DRESSING

Add ketchup and relish to the above to taste.

CITRUS DRESSING

¼ c. pineapple juice
1 tbsp. orange juice
½ tsp. salt
½ c. corn or peanut oil

In cup, combine ingredients.

SWEET LEMON DRESSING

2 tsp. lemon juice
4 tsp. honey
6 tbsp. olive oil

In cup, combine ingredients.

SOUR CARAWAY DRESSING

⅓ c. sour cream   1 tbsp. lemon juice
½ tbsp. caraway seeds   ½ tsp. salt
1 tbsp. sesame seeds   Dash pepper

In bowl, combine ingredients.

SAUCES

CREAMY BROWN GRAVY

2 tbsp. unbleached white flour	**2 tbsp. corn or peanut oil**
	1 tbsp. soy sauce
	1 vegetable bouillon cube
	1 c. warm water

In saucepan, mix, flour, oil, and soy sauce over low flame, stirring rapidly.

In cup, dissolve bouillon cube in water.

Stir bouillon rapidly into flour mixture, so that lumps do not form. Continue stirring until gravy is smooth.

Note: If you are storing gravy, keep in a closed container in fridge. By the time you are ready to use it again, it will probably be quite solid. If this happens, dump it into a saucepan with enough water to create a creamy mixture again, and stir.

WHEAT-GERM SAUCE

2 tbsp. unbleached white flour	**2 tbsp. corn or peanut oil**
1 c. milk	**¼ c. water**
1 tbsp. wheat germ	**3 tsp. salt**

In pan, over low flame, combine flour and oil.

Add milk, water, wheat germ, and salt, a little at a time, stirring constantly to avoid lumps.

⚘ MAIN COURSES

BEANS, PEAS, etc.

BEAN CURD SUKIYAKI

¼ c. scallions, chopped
2 c. bean curds*
⅓ c. mushrooms, sliced
1 c. bean sprouts
1 green pepper, cored
  and chopped
1 c. Chinese cabbage,
  sliced
3 c. spinach, washed
  well and chopped

Oil for cooking
½ tsp. powdered ginger
2 tbsp. soy sauce
2 tbsp. water

Cover bottom of large pan with oil and sauté ginger for 1 min.
Add scallions and sauté 3 mins. Add all other vegetables, mixing lightly.
In cup, combine soy sauce and water. Pour over vegetables. Cover. Cook over low flame for 5 to 7 mins.

* Dice if commercial. If not, it will be in curd form and not squares.

CHAFF AND BEANS

½ c. black beans,
cooked
2½ c. soy chaff (please
see p. 15)
1 c. mushrooms,
chopped

2 tbsp. corn or peanut
oil
2 tbsp. soy sauce
1 tbsp. cornstarch or
½ tbsp. arrowroot
1 c. water

In pan, sauté chaff and mushrooms in oil over low flame for 7 mins., making sure not to burn.

In bowl, mash beans and add them to contents of pan.

Dissolve cornstarch in mixture of water and soy sauce. Pour over chaff and beans. Cover and cook over low flame for 20 mins.

CHICK-PEA CHOPS

2 c. chick-peas, soaked
overnight
1 large onion, minced
4 pieces rye or whole
wheat bread, with-
out crusts and torn
in pieces
¼ c. milk

¼ c. water
½ tsp. pepper
1 tsp. garlic powder
1 tsp. salt
Butter for baking dish
1 tsp. sesame seeds
(optional)

Drain peas.

Run peas, onion, and bread through grinder or chop in blender.

In bowl, mix the above with the other ingredients (except butter). Form into ten medium-sized fairly flat patties. Preheat oven to 350°. Arrange patties in well-buttered baking dish. Bake for ½ hr. or until tops are lightly crusted.

CHICK-PEA LOAF

1 c. chick-peas, cooked	Water (enough to cover
1 c. celery, diced	saucepan bottom)
1 c. cauliflower, diced	¼ tsp. soy sauce
½ green pepper, diced	¼ tsp. thyme
2 tbsp. whole wheat	½ c. water
flour	Oil for baking pan
	¼ tsp. marjoram
	(optional)

In covered saucepan, steam celery, cauliflower, and green pepper in about 1″ of water until tender. Drain. In bowl, mash chick-peas with celery, cauliflower. and green pepper.

Dilute flour in ½ c. water. Mix flour, water, soy sauce, and spices with vegetables.

Preheat oven to 350°.

Oil baking pan. Spoon mixture into oiled pan. Bake for 30 to 45 mins. until top is crusted over.

Serve with gravy (please see p. 48). Makes 4 small portions.

GINGER-BEAN MIX

⅓ c. scallions, sliced
1 tomato, chopped
¼ c. grated coconut
1 c. soybeans, cooked
and mashed
3 tbsp. whole wheat
flour

½ tsp. powdered ginger
2 tbsp. corn or peanut
oil
1½ tsp. cornstarch or
½ tsp. arrowroot
1 c. pineapple juice
1 tbsp. soy sauce
¼ c. warm water

In pan, sauté scallions, ginger, tomato, and coconut in oil for 3 mins. Add soybeans. Cook for 3 mins.

In cup, dissolve cornstarch and flour in pineapple juice, soy sauce, and water. Add to pan. Cover. Cook over low flame for 10 mins.

LENTIL LOAF

1 c. lentils, cooked
1 med. onion, peeled
and sliced
1 med. tomato, diced
1½ c. bread crumbs
1 tbsp. Parmesan
cheese, grated
½ c. milk

1 tbsp. corn or peanut
oil
¼ tsp. garlic powder
1 tsp. salt
Oil for loaf pan

In frying pan, sauté onion and tomato in oil until onion yellows and tomato becomes soft.

In bowl, mash lentils. Add onion and tomato. Mix in garlic powder, salt, milk, and 1 c. bread crumbs.

Preheat oven to 350°.
Oil loaf pan. Spoon mixture into pan. Sprinkle remaining bread crumbs over top. Bake for ½ hr. Serve with gravy (please see p. 48).

NOODLES AND DUMPLINGS

BLINTZES

1¼ c. unbleached white flour	1 c. water
½ c. sour cream	1 tbsp. corn or peanut oil
½ c. milk	1 tbsp. salt
	2 tbsp. cornstarch or 1 tbsp. arrowroot
	Butter for frying and baking

In bowl, beat until smooth all ingredients except butter. In frying pan, melt just enough butter to cover bottom of pan. When butter is hot (turning brown but not burning), pour a thin layer of blintze batter into pan. When bubbles form on top of batter, carefully turn blintze over. When both sides are brown, remove. Drain on paper. Makes 8 blintzes.

BLINTZE FILLINGS

2 c. ricotta cheese or, if you can't get that, pot cheese	1 tsp. salt
	1 tsp. water

In bowl, cream ingredients together.

VARIATIONS

For sweet filling—add 3 tbsp. fruit preserves or jam to cheese.

For spicy filling—add 2 tbsp. finely chopped scallions to cheese.

Spoon 1 tbsp. of filling onto edge of each blintze. Roll blintzes up.

Preheat oven to 350°.

Butter baking dish and place filled blintzes inside. Bake for 10 mins.

FAR EASTERN DUMPLINGS

DUMPLINGS

2 c. whole wheat flour	**1 tsp. salt**
Flour for rolling	**⅔ c. water**

In bowl, combine the 2 c. of flour, salt, and water. Knead for 5 mins., pressing fists into dough and turning it. Return to bowl. Let stand, covered, for ½ hr.

Flour board or tabletop and roll out mixture until thin. Cut into squares approximately 3″ x 3″.

FILLING

1 c. soybeans, cooked and mashed	**1 tbsp. chives, chopped**
¼ c. green pepper, minced	**1 tbsp. fresh parsley, chopped**
½ c. water chestnuts, minced	

In bowl, combine ingredients.

Place 2 tbsp. filling on each dough square. Fold

corners of dough to meet in center. Seal edges with a little water.

Either steam dumplings for 15 mins. in pot in about 1″ of water over low flame or fry in corn or peanut oil, browning on both sides. My house prefers the fried version.

LINGUINE AND ALMONDS

SAUCE

2 heaping tbsp. un- bleached white flour	2 tbsp. corn or peanut oil 1 vegetable bouillon cube 1½ c. warm water ½ tsp. salt 1 tbsp. fresh parsley

In pan, over low heat, combine flour and oil, stirring.

In cup, dissolve bouillon cube in water and add to flour mixture, stirring briskly so that lumps don't form. When smooth, stir in salt and parsley.

(Double this recipe for a larger amount of linguine than given below.)

NOODLES

½ to ¾ lb. linguine, cooked
½ c. almonds, blanched and halved length- wise
2 tbsp. cottage cheese

In bowl, combine linguine, almonds, and cottage cheese with sauce.

MACAO NOODLES AND VEGETABLES

⅓ c. onion, sliced
2 c. mushrooms, sliced
2 c. spinach, washed
  well and chopped
2 c. turnips, sliced in
  matchsticks*
1 c. carrots, sliced in
  matchsticks*
½ c. bean sprouts
¼ c. bamboo shoots
⅓ c. water chestnuts,
  sliced
½ c. walnuts, chopped
3 c. noodles, cooked

¼ c. corn or peanut oil
¼ c. water
¼ c. soy sauce
1 tbsp. cornstarch or
  ½ tbsp. arrowroot
1 tsp. MSG**
1 c. bean curd, diced
  and fried in 2 tbsp.
  oil (optional)

In pan, sauté onions and mushrooms in oil for 5 mins. Add other vegetables and walnuts, and cook, stirring, for 3 mins. Add noodles.

Dissolve cornstarch and MSG in mixture of soy sauce and water. Add to pan. Cover. Cook over low flame for 10 mins.

* To get a matchstick shape, slice vegetables fairly thin lengthwise and then lengthwise again.

** A lot of people are very down on MSG (monosodium glutamate), saying it can do funny things to your head. Personally, I have never felt any ill effects from consumption of MSG, but I thought it fair to warn you of other people's thing.

MACARONI AND VEGETABLES

1 large onion, chopped	1 tbsp. olive oil
½ c. pine nuts	1 tbsp. butter
½ c. yellow or black	2 tsp. salt
raisins	2 tsp. lime juice
2 plum tomatoes,	
sliced	
3 c. broccoli, chopped	
2 c. macaroni, cooked	
2 tbsp. sesame seeds	

In pan, sauté onions, pine nuts, raisins, and sesame seeds in oil and butter for 3 mins. Add tomatoes. Cook for 7 mins. over low flame. Add broccoli, macaroni, lime juice, and salt. Cover. Cook for 10 mins. over low flame.

MAMA ROBERTA'S LASAGNA

SAUCE

1 c. onions, chopped	4 tbsp. olive oil
large	Juice of ½ lemon
½ c. carrots, chopped	¼ tsp. celery salt
fine	¼ tsp. basil
½ c. celery, chopped	¼ tsp. thyme
(tops too)	½ tsp. marjoram
8 tomatoes, puréed*	1½ tsp. allspice
¾ c. tomato paste	½ tbsp. salt
1½ c. mushrooms,	¼ tsp. black pepper
sliced	2 tbsp. raw sugar
	¼ tsp. garlic, minced
	1½ tbsp. parsley,
	chopped

* To purée tomatoes, boil them in water 5 mins. Peel, mash.

In pot, sauté onion, garlic, carrots, and celery in 2 tbsp. oil for 7 mins. Sprinkle with half of the lemon juice. Add celery salt and parsley, stirring lightly. Add puréed tomatoes, stirring.

Stir in remaining ingredients, except for mushrooms, remaining lemon juice, and remaining oil. Cover. Cook over low flame for 4 to 6 hrs. If sauce gets too thick, add up to ¾ c. water, stirring well.

After 2 to 3 hrs. of cooking, brown the mushrooms in pan in 2 tbsp. oil. Stir into sauce with rest of lemon juice.

Noodles

20 lasagna noodles
  (about 8" x 2"),
  cooked
2 c. ricotta cheese or
  fine-curd cottage
  cheese
2 c. Mozzarella cheese,
  sliced thin
¼ c. Parmesan cheese,
  grated fine

Oil for baking dish
1 c. spinach, chopped
  (optional)

In oiled baking pan, arrange an overlapping layer of noodles. Mix sauce with ricotta. Smooth over noodles. Top with a few slices of Mozzarella. Sprinkle with Parmesan and spinach. Continue arranging such layers until ingredients are exhausted.

Preheat oven to 350°.

Bake for 20 mins.

WHOLE WHEAT ROLL, FILLED

ROLL

1 c. whole wheat flour	⅓ c. water
Flour for rolling	1 tsp. salt

In bowl, combine flour, water, and salt. Knead for 2 mins.

Return to bowl, cover, let stand ½ hr.

Flour board or tabletop and roll out mixture until thin. Cut into squares approximately 5″ x 5″.

FILLING

½ c. bean curd	1 tsp. salt
½ c. celery, minced	2 tbsp. corn or peanut
½ c. water chestnuts,	oil
minced	1 tbsp. soy sauce
½ c. scallions	

In bowl, combine bean curd, celery, chestnuts, scallions, and salt.

In frying pan sauté for 3 mins. in oil. Add soy sauce.

Place 2 tbsp. filling on one end of each dough square. Roll up dough.

In frying pan, deep-fry rolls in hot oil until brown and crisp.* Drain. Makes 6 rolls.

* When deep-frying, make sure oil is hot enough by seeing if water drops sputter on it.

NUTS

CASHEW FRENCH TOAST

¼ c. almonds, blanched   Butter for browning
¼ c. cashews
4 to 6 pieces bread
 1 tbsp. sesame seeds
½ c. milk

In grinder or blender, combine sesame seeds, nuts, and milk. Pour above mixture into bowl. Soak bread in mixture about 5 mins.
  In frying pan, melt enough butter to cover bottom of pan. Brown each slice of bread on both sides (adding butter whenever necessary).
  Serve with maple syrup or cinnamon.

GRAINS

BARLEY AND MUSHROOMS

2 c. mushrooms, sliced   2 tbsp. butter
3 scallions, chopped   1 vegetable bouillon
1 c. pearl barley   cube
                         3½ c. water
                         2 tsp. dill weed
                         2 tbsp. soy sauce

In pot, sauté mushrooms and scallions in butter for 5 mins.

In cup, dissolve bouillon cube in 1 c. water. Pour all water into pot. When water boils, add barley, dill, and soy sauce, stirring. Cover. Cook for 15 to 20 mins. over medium flame until water is absorbed. Serve with sour cream.

PILAU RICE

1 med. onion, chopped	5 tbsp. butter
½ c. raisins	¼ tsp. chili powder
1 tbsp. pine nuts	2 tsp. salt
1½ c. raw rice	¼ tsp. powdered car-
1 c. yoghurt	damon
	½ tsp. powdered
	ginger
	2 tsp. mustard seeds
	3¼ c. water
	1 clove garlic, minced

In pot, sauté onion, garlic, raisins, nuts, salt, and spices in butter for 5 mins.

Add rice, and continue to sauté, over low flame, stirring, for 7 mins.

Add yoghurt. Pour in water. Cover. Cook over low flame until rice is done (about 15 mins.).

POTATO-PEA PILAU

1 c. raw rice	3 to 4 tbsp. ghee
1 med. potato, peeled	2 tsp. salt
and cut in chunks	2¼ c. water
1 c. peas	

In saucepan, melt ghee. Stir in rice, and cook until it turns yellow (about 7 mins.).
Stir in potato chunks, peas, and salt. Pour in water. Cover. Cook over low flame until water is absorbed (10 to 15 mins.). Stir.

SUPER RICE

2 c. raw white rice	4 c. water
2 tbsp. pine nuts	3 tbsp. butter
¼ c. raisins	¼ c. honey

In saucepan, cook rice in 3 c. water until water is absorbed (15 mins.).
In pan, brown nuts and raisins in butter, making sure not to burn. (Keep stirring.)
Stir in rice and let it turn yellow.
Dissolve honey in remaining 1 c. water. Pour over rice. Stir. Cook until water is absorbed.

TOMATO-RICE LOAF

1 med. tomato, sliced	1 tbsp. oil
1 stalk celery, sliced	1 tsp. garlic powder
2 c. rice, cooked	2 tsp. onion powder
½ c. bread crumbs	Oil for loaf pan
1 c. milk	

In pan, sauté tomato and celery in oil. Add garlic and onion powders, rice, crumbs, and milk.
Spoon above mixture into well-oiled loaf pan.
Preheat oven to 350°. Bake for ½ hr.

UPMA

1 med. onion, peeled
and sliced
½ c. broccoli or cauli-
flower, chopped
½ c. carrots, chopped
1 tbsp. cashew nuts,
halved rectangularly
2 tbsp. almonds,
blanched and halved
rectangularly
1 tbsp. raisins
2 c. farina or Cream of
Wheat

2 tbsp. oil
2 tbsp. salt
1 tbsp. curry powder
1 tbsp. mustard seeds
4 c. water
2 tbsp. butter

In pot, heat oil till hot. Sauté salt, carry powder, and mustard seeds until seeds start to pop.

Add onion and cook until it turns yellow.

Add other vegetables, nuts, and raisins, and cook for 4 mins. over low flame.

Turn up flame, pour in water, and bring to a boil.

When boiling, pour in farina, in a smooth, steady stream, stirring rapidly and constantly. When mixture is firm, smooth over top and melt butter on it.

Note: To make perfect Upma, you must be very careful when pouring the farina. Never dump all of it in at once, or sticky, uncooked lumps will form. The smooth consistency can be acquired only by constant rapid stirring as you pour. Also, to avoid splattering farina all over yourself, turn down the flame just before you start to pour.

VARIATION

Top Upma with grated cheese and apple slices. Bake at 250° until cheese melts and begins to brown.

VEGETABLES AND FRUITS

BANANA CURRY

4 slightly underripe bananas (with skins left on), cut in 1" pieces	1 tbsp. butter
	½ tsp. caraway seeds
	½ tsp. turmeric
1 tbsp. milk	½ tsp. salt
	½ tsp. curry powder
	½ tsp. chili powder (optional)
	1 tbsp. lemon juice

In frying pan, melt butter. Sauté caraway seeds and turmeric for 5 mins.

Add bananas and brown on both sides about 2 mins.

Add salt, curry, and chili (if using) and sauté for 3 to 5 mins.

Add milk and lemon juice. Cover, and cook until bananas are tender but not falling apart.

BAKED CHEDDAR SQUASH

1 large acorn squash	2 tbsp. butter
1 c. Cheddar cheese, grated	Melted butter for baking dish
1 c. bread crumbs	

In pot, steam squash in about 1″ water until skin and seeds can be easily removed. Brush baking dish with melted butter. Mash squash and spoon into baking dish. Preheat oven to 350°. Sprinkle cheese over squash. Sprinkle crumbs over cheese. Dot crumbs with butter. Bake for 20 mins. or until cheese bubbles. Mix squash, cheese, and crumbs together before serving.

BAKED EGGPLANT MERF AND MILDRED

1 med. eggplant,	**Water for cooking**
peeled	**2 tsp. garlic powder**
¼ to ½ c. bread crumbs	**Salt to taste**
1 c. American cheese,	**Butter for baking dish**
diced	

Slice eggplant. Cook until tender in enough water to cover. Drain. Mash well.

Preheat oven to 350°.

In bowl, mix mashed eggplant with garlic powder, salt, and bread crumbs.

Spoon into buttered baking dish. Cover with diced American cheese. Bake for 30 mins.

CHEDDAR CHEESE PIE

CRUST

2 c. unbleached white flour	1 tsp. salt
½ c. Cheddar cheese, grated	⅔ c. water
Flour for kneading	Oil for baking dish

In bowl, combine flour and salt. Stir in cheese and water.

Knead dough until firm on well-floured board or tabletop.

Roll dough until thin.

Fit dough into well-oiled pie plate.

FILLING

1 c. peas, cooked	½ tsp. salt
1 c. corn kernels, uncooked	½ tsp. paprika
⅓ c. cottage cheese	
1 c. Cheddar cheese, grated	
1 tbsp. unbleached white flour	
1 c. wheat germ	

In bowl, combine all ingredients except wheat germ.
Preheat oven to 350°.

Spoon filling mixture onto dough. Sprinkle wheat germ over top. Bake for 30 mins. or until crust is firm.

DICED EGGPLANT

1 med. eggplant, diced
1 onion, peeled and
   sliced
1 green pepper, cored
   and chopped
¼ c. pine nuts
¼ c. almonds, blanched
   and cut in half
   lengthwise
1 tomato, sliced
¼ c. bread crumbs
¼ c. Parmesan cheese,
   grated fine

2 tbsp. oil
1 tbsp. butter
2 tsp. salt
1 tbsp. lime juice

In pan, sauté eggplant, onion, and pepper in oil and butter for 15 mins. Add other ingredients. Cover. Cook over low flame for 10 to 15 mins.

EGGPLANT CURRY

1 medium-size egg-
   plant
2 med. onions, sliced
½ c. coconut or regular
   milk

1 tsp. lemon juice
1 tsp. ground mustard
1 tsp. salt
1 tsp. curry powder
2 tbsp. butter
3 tsp. peanut or coco-
   nut oil
1 tsp. chili powder (op-
   tional)
½ tsp. fresh ginger,
   chopped (optional)

In pot, boil eggplant for 6 mins. Then drain and dice. In frying pan, sauté onions, lemon juice, and spices in butter for 10 mins. Add eggplant and sauté for another 5 mins. Add oil and milk, cover, and cook until most of the liquid is gone.

EGGPLANT PARMIGIANA

1 large eggplant
2½ c. tomatoes, chopped
2 c. green pepper, cored and chopped
1 med. onion, peeled and sliced
8 oz. Mozzarella cheese, sliced
¾ c. Parmesan cheese, grated
1 c. unbleached white flour

2 cloves garlic, minced
¼ tsp. garlic powder
2 tsp. salt
½ tsp. pepper
¼ tsp. basil
Olive oil for frying and baking pan
Water for soaking eggplant

In pot, steam eggplant in about 1″ of water for about 20 mins. or until it can easily be pierced by a fork. Drain. Slice into medium pieces. Place slices in enough water to cover.

In bowl, mix flour, garlic powder, 1 tsp. salt, and ¼ tsp. pepper. Dip eggplant slices in flour mixture.

In frying pan, heat enough oil to cover bottom of pan. Fry eggplant slices until brown on both sides. If oil in pan gets absorbed, pour in more oil. Drain eggplant.

In oiled baking pan, arrange eggplant slices. Cover with slices of Mozzarella. Sprinkle Parmesan cheese over top.

In same frying pan, cook tomatoes, pepper, onion, garlic, ¼ tsp. pepper, and 1 tsp. salt, covered, over low flame until a nice liquidy sauce is formed. Preheat oven to 350°. Pour sauce over eggplant and cheese. Bake for ½ hour.

FRUIT-POTATO CASSEROLE

3 med. sweet potatoes	3 tbsp. butter
2 med. Rome apples,	½ c. honey
peeled and sliced	½ c. warm orange juice
2 bananas, peeled and	1 tsp. cornstarch or ½
sliced in 1″ pieces	tsp. arrowroot
	2 tsp. cinnamon
	Oil for baking dish

In pot, boil potatoes (in enough water to cover) until tender but not mushy. Drain. Peel and slice. Oil baking dish well.

Arrange potato slices in dish. Dot with butter. Brush with honey. Cover with a layer of apple slices, buttered and honeyed. Cover with a layer of banana slices, buttered and honeyed.

Preheat oven to 350°.

Dissolve cornstarch well in orange juice. Pour orange juice and any leftover honey and butter over banana layer. Sprinkle cinnamon over top. Bake for 30 to 45 mins. until banana layer is brown but not burned. Baste once or twice with orange juice.

KASHMIRIAN CAULIFLOWER AND CABBAGE

2 c. cauliflower, cut into flowerettes	1 tbsp. mustard seeds
1 c. cabbage, chopped	¼ tsp. turmeric
3 tbsp. yoghurt	¼ tsp. powdered cloves
	¼ tsp. pepper
	¼ tsp. cumin powder
	¼ tsp. cinnamon
	3 tbsp. corn or peanut oil

In pan, sauté mustard seeds and spices in oil until seeds begin to pop.
Add cauliflower and cabbage, and sauté, stirring, for 3 mins.
Stir in yoghurt. Cover. Simmer for 7 mins.

POTATO CURRY

4 c. potatoes, peeled and diced	1 tsp. ground mustard
2 med. onions, peeled and sliced	1 tsp. salt
½ c. coconut or regular milk	1 tsp. curry powder
	3 tsp. coconut or peanut oil
	1 tsp. lemon juice
	2 tbsp. butter
	1 tsp. chili powder (optional)
	½ tsp. fresh ginger (optional)

Boil potatoes in a pot for 6 mins. Remove.
In frying pan, sauté onions, spices, and lemon juice

in butter for 10 mins. Add oil and potatoes and continue cooking for 5 mins. Add milk. Cook uncovered until liquid is almost gone.

SMOKY BROCCOLI

4 c. broccoli, chopped	Oil for baking dish
2 med. tomatoes, chopped	
1 c. smoked cheese or Provolone, grated	
1 c. almonds, blanched	
2 c. yoghurt	

In bowl, blend all ingredients except oil. Preheat oven to 350°. Spoon mixture into oiled baking dish. Bake for 20 mins.

SOYBEAN-TOMATO MIX
(*or to Carry Another Step*)
STUFFED PEPPERS

2 med. tomatoes, diced	2 tbsp. corn or peanut oil
1 c. onions, peeled and chopped	1 tbsp. soy sauce
¼ c. raisins	¼ tsp. chili pepper, mashed
2 c. soy chaff (please see p. 15)	Oil for cooking
4 large green peppers	
2 tsp. sesame seeds	

In frying pan, sauté tomatoes, onions, raisins, and sesame seeds in 2 tbsp. oil until onions are yellow (5 to 7 mins.) Add soy chaff, soy sauce, and chili pepper and continue to cook for 3 mins., stirring.
Cut peppers in half lengthwise; remove seeds and membrane. Stuff mix into ½ peppers.
Cover bottom of frying pan with oil. Arrange peppers in pan. Cover. Cook over low to medium flame until peppers are soft (about ½ hr.). Make sure not to burn.

SPINACH-WHEAT CROQUETTES

½ c. bulgur	1 c. water
2 c. spinach, chopped	¼ tsp. cayenne pepper
½ c. Muenster cheese, grated	1 tsp. salt
	Oil for deep frying
2 tbsp. whole wheat flour	

In pot, cook bulgur in water.
In bowl, combine all ingredients. Roll mixture into tablespoon-size balls.
Heat about 2″ of oil in deep-frying pan. When oil is very hot, fry croquettes until brown all over. Drain well.

STUFFED CABBAGE

½ c. couscous
8 cabbage leaves, boiled
   tender*
¼ c. raisins
1 c. mushrooms,
   chopped
1 small onion, chopped
1 small tomato,
   chopped
Sour cream for topping

2 c. water
1 tbsp. corn or peanut
   oil
1 tbsp. butter
½ tsp. cinnamon
2½ tbsp. honey
1 vegetable bouillon
   cube
Oil for baking pan

In saucepan, cook couscous in 1 c. water until done (about 3 to 5 mins.). In pan, sauté raisins, mushrooms, onion, and tomato in oil and butter for 5 mins. Stir in couscous, cinnamon, and 1½ tbsp. honey.

Place a tablespoon of mixture on edge of each cabbage leaf. Roll up. Tie a piece of string around leaf to hold in place.

Preheat oven to 350°.

Arrange stuffed leaves in oiled baking dish.

In cup, dissolve bouillon cube and remaining honey in 1 c. warm water. Pour over leaves. Bake for 15 mins.

Serve with sour cream.

* It is difficult to remove leaves from cabbage unless the cabbage is boiled. If you have no use for a whole boiled cabbage, cut out the core of the cabbage and then carefully remove 8 large leaves. Wrap the rest of the cabbage and store in fridge.

STUFFED MUSHROOMS MAO

20 med. mushrooms, washed	1 vegetable bouillon cube
½ c. bean curd, mashed	2 tsp. cornstarch or
½ med. onion, peeled and minced	1 tsp. arrowroot
2 stalks celery, minced	¾ c. warm water

Remove stems from mushrooms. Chop stems.

In bowl, combine stems with bean curd, onion, and celery.

Stuff mixture into mushroom caps. Arrange stuffed mushrooms in frying pan.

In cup, dissolve bouillon cube and cornstarch in water. Pour into pan. Cover. Cook over low flame for 15 mins.

STUFFED MUSHROOMS FABRIZIO

20 med. mushrooms	3 garlic cloves, minced
½ c. bread crumbs	½ c. parsley, chopped
½ c. Parmesan cheese, grated	1 tbsp. butter
	1 tbsp. olive oil
	1 tsp. salt
	½ tsp. pepper
	Oil for pan

Remove stems from mushrooms. Chop stems.

In pan, sauté garlic and parsley in butter and oil

for 5 mins. Mix in stems, bread crumbs, Parmesan cheese, salt, and pepper. Stuff mushroom caps with the mixture.
Preheat oven to 350°.
Arrange stuffed mushrooms in well-oiled baking pan. Bake for 20 mins.

SUBTLE CHEESE-VEGETABLE DISH

1 small head cauliflower, broken into flowerettes	3 tbsp. corn or peanut oil
2 c. string beans, cut in half at an angle	2 tsp. cornstarch or 1 tsp. arrowroot
1 c. Muenster cheese, diced well	5 tbsp. water 3 tbsp. soy sauce ½ tsp. paprika

In heavy pan, heat oil. Sauté cauliflower and beans for 5 mins.
Add cornstarch, water, soy sauce, and paprika. Lower flame, cover, cook for 7 mins.
Sprinkle cheese over top. Cover and cook for 20 mins.

SWEET AND SOUR VEGETABLES

2 c. bean curd*	⅓ c. corn or peanut oil
1 c. pineapple, minced	2 tsp. salt
2 c. tomatoes, diced	¼ c. warm soy sauce
⅔ c. scallions, chopped	1 tbsp. cornstarch or
½ c. almonds, blanched	1½ tsp. arrowroot

* If you are using commercial bean curd, which usually comes in squares, dice for this recipe. If using homemade curd, simply mix in.

In pan, sauté bean curd and scallions in oil for 3 mins.
Dissolve cornstarch and salt in soy sauce. Add to
pan.
Add tomatoes and cook for 5 mins.
Add pineapple and almonds and cook for 2 mins.

TOMATO CURRY

1 med. onion, peeled and sliced	2 tbsp. corn or peanut oil
2 large tomatoes, sliced	1 tsp. salt
	½ tsp. turmeric
	¼ tsp chili powder
	¼ c. water (about)
	1 garlic clove, minced

In pan, sauté salt and spices in oil for 1 min. Add onion
and garlic and cook for 3 mins.
Add tomato and cook for 5 mins.
Add water. Cover. Cook over low flame for 7 mins.

VEGETABLE ROAST

½ c. onion, peeled and
  minced
1 c. celery, minced
1½ c. carrots, ground
  or chopped in
  blender
½ c. green pepper,
  minced after center
  is removed
1½ c. string beans,
  ground or chopped
  in blender

1 c. peas, steamed
6 tbsp. wheat germ
1 tbsp. sesame seeds

4 tbsp. butter
1 tbsp. arrowroot or
2 tbsp. cornstarch
1½ tsp. warm soy sauce
1 tbsp. corn or pea-
nut oil
Oil for baking pan
2 c. Chinese dry
noodles (optional)

In frying pan, in butter, sauté onion, celery, carrots, and green pepper for 15 mins.

Dissolve cornstarch in soy sauce.

Add other ingredients, except noodles and oil, and sauté for 3 more mins.

Preheat oven to 350°.

Oil baking pan. Spoon in mixture. Crumble noodles on top. Bake for ½ hr.

WESTHAMPTON BEACH STEW

1 large onion, peeled
and sliced
2 sweet potatoes,
sliced
1 small squash (acorn
or yellow), steamed
tender and peeled
3 carrots, peeled and
sliced
3 stalks celery, sliced

1 large tomato, cut in
   chunks
3 parsnips, peeled and
   sliced
½ c. corn kernels
1 c. peas

2 tbsp. butter
1 vegetable bouillon
   cube
2 tsp. cornstarch or
   1 tsp. arrowroot
1 c. warm water
2 tsp. dill weed
½ tsp. pepper
1 bay leaf
1 tbsp. fresh parsley,
   chopped

In pot, sauté onion in butter for 5 mins. Add all other vegetables and parsley.

In cup, dissolve bouillon cube and cornstarch in water. Add to pot.

Stir in dill weed, pepper, and bay leaf. Cover. Simmer over low flame for ½ hr. or until vegetables are tender (not mushy).

MISCELLANEOUS

RAMA'S YOGA PIZZA

DOUGH

3½ c. whole wheat flour	1½ c. water
8 oz. Bonbel, Gouda,	1 cake yeast
or Mozzarella cheese,	1 tsp. garlic powder
sliced thin	1 tsp. salt
½ c. Parmesan cheese,	2 tbsp. oil
grated	Oil for baking pan

In bowl, dissolve yeast in lukewarm water.
In another bowl, combine flour, garlic powder, and salt. Add dissolved yeast.
Knead dough on floured board or tabletop for 5 mins. Add oil and form dough into a ball.
Place ball in bowl. Cover. Keep in warm place about 2 hrs. till dough has almost doubled.

SAUCE

1 heaping c. mush-rooms, sliced	1 garlic clove, minced
	¼ tsp. basil
1 large green pepper, cored and chopped	½ c. parsley, chopped
	1 tbsp. butter
3 c. plum tomatoes, chopped	2 tbsp. olive oil
	1 tsp. salt

In pan, sauté garlic, basil, and mushrooms in butter and oil for 5 mins.

Add pepper, parsley, and tomatoes. Stir in salt. Cover. Cook over low flame for 45 mins.

Preheat oven to 350°.

Place dough on oiled pizza pan or cookie sheet, stretching dough all over pan.

Arrange cheese slices over dough. Pour sauce over slices. Sprinkle Parmesan over sauce. Bake for ½ hr. Turn oven to low. Bake for 15 mins. more.

🌷 SIDE DISHES

Serve with soup or main course.

CHUTNEY

7 med. tomatoes	1 c. vinegar
3 med. apples	1 c. brown sugar
½ c. raisins	¼ c. molasses
1 c. dried figs, chopped	1½ tsp. salt
	½ tsp. pepper
	½ tsp. cinnamon
	½ tsp. chili powder
	½ tsp. ground cloves
	½ tsp. ground coriander
	½ tsp. ground ginger

In large pot of boiling water, parboil tomatoes and apples for 5 mins. Drain. Peel and dice. (Skin will come off quite easily with this method.)

In saucepan, combine vinegar, sugar, molasses, salt, and spices, and cook over medium flame, stirring. Add raisins, figs, tomatoes, and apples. Cover and cook over low flame for 1 hr.

Keep chutney in airtight container in refrigerator.

FLORENTINE BEANS

1 lb. string beans, cut in half lengthwise	2 tbsp. olive oil
	1 tsp. salt
¼ c. almonds, blanched and split lengthwise	1 clove garlic, minced
1 tbsp. sesame seeds	

In saucepan, steam beans in about 1" of water until semisoft.

In frying pan, sauté garlic, sesame seeds, and almonds in oil for 5 mins. over low flame.

Add string beans and salt and cook, covered, for 7 mins.

This makes 4 small portions. For larger portions, increase accordingly.

FRIED ARTICHOKE HEARTS

4 artichokes	⅓ c. oil
⅓ c. unbleached white flour	Salt to taste
	Water for soaking

In pot, steam artichokes in about 1″ of water until tender.

Separate the outer leaves from the heart. When you reach the fuzzy matter around the inner core, scrape it off before preparing hearts. (Wow, it sounds like an anatomy course.)

Soak hearts in enough water to cover for about 5 mins. Dip into flour.

In pan, heat oil very hot. Fry hearts in oil until brown.

Add salt.

BUTTER SAUCE

    2 sticks (½ lb.) butter
    1 tsp. garlic powder
    Salt to taste

In saucepan, combine above ingredients over low flame, stirring.

Dip fried hearts and steamed leaves in butter sauce.

Note: If you have never eaten artichokes before, strip the tender or lower part of each leaf from the leaf itself, with your teeth. Don't just eat the leaves whole.

GINGERED BROCCOLI

**1 bunch broccoli,
  washed, separated
  into individual
  stalks and then cut
  lengthwise**

**½ tsp. ginger powder
2 tbsp. corn or peanut
  oil
1 tbsp. honey
1 tbsp. soy sauce
¼ c. warm water**

In pan, sauté ginger in oil for 1 min. Add broccoli and cook for 5 mins. In cup, dilute honey in soy sauce and water. Pour over broccoli. Cover. Cook over low flame for 10 mins.

JEWISH SOUL FOOD—TZIMMES

3 c. apples, grated
3 c. carrots, grated
¼ c. almonds, blanched
and chopped, or
¼ c. cashews,
chopped, or ¼ c.
pine nuts, chopped,
or a mixture

3 tbsp. butter
¾ c. water
2 tbsp. honey
½ tsp. cinnamon

In saucepan, melt butter. Add other ingredients. Cover and cook over low flame for about 60 to 75 mins. Make sure mixture doesn't burn.

RAITA

½ c. plain yoghurt
½ cucumber, peeled
and minced

½ tsp. salt
¼ tsp. powdered cori-
ander
¼ tsp. cumin powder

In bowl, combine ingredients. Serve with curry dishes.

SWEET POTATO MASH

4 large sweet potatoes	Water for boiling
1 med. onion, peeled	1 tbsp. mustard seeds
and chopped	2 tbsp. butter

In pot, boil potatoes in water until soft. Drain and peel.
In frying pan, sauté onion in butter until yellow.
Add mustard seeds and cook until they begin to pop.
In bowl, mash potatoes and add onion mixture.
This recipe can be used to make Pinapotato Soup.
(See p. 35.)

SEPTEMBER SQUASH

1 small onion, sliced	3 tbsp. butter
1 large yellow squash,	Salt to taste
cut in 1″ pieces	Pepper to taste
2 tbsp. almonds,	
blanched and	
slivered	

In large frying pan, sauté onion in butter for 5 mins.
Add squash and nuts. Cover, and cook over low
flame for 15 mins or until squash is tender. Add salt
and pepper.

🌸 DESSERTS AND MUNCHIES

ALMOND HALWA

1 c. semolina	4 tbsp. butter
½ c. almonds, blanched and chopped	2 c. water
	1 c. maple syrup

In saucepan, melt butter. Add semolina, stirring. When semolina is yellow, add water, syrup, and almonds. Stir mixture constantly over medium heat until it solidifies so that lumps do not form. Cool and cut into squares.

APPLE SNAP

2 large Rome apples	¾ c. sweet butter
13 graham crackers	1 c. brown sugar
¼ c. raisins	3 tsp. cinnamon
	Butter for loaf pan

In bowl, cream together butter and brown sugar. Crumble 10 crackers into this mixture. Spread half of this mixture over bottom of well-buttered loaf pan.

Slice apples into portions ⅛″ thick.

Preheat oven to 365°.

Arrange a layer of apple slices over cracker mixture. Sprinkle 1 crumbled cracker, 1 tsp. cinnamon, and a few raisins over apples. Cover with another layer of apple slices, cracker, cinnamon, and raisins. Repeat again.

Spread second half of butter and sugar mixture over top. Bake for 30 to 35 mins.

COUNTRY PIE

CRUST

¼ c. graham cracker crumbs	⅓ c. corn or peanut oil
⅓ c. cornmeal	1 tbsp. honey
½ c. wheat germ	2 tbsp. molasses

In bowl, combine ingredients. Press into pie plate. Chill in freezer section of refrigerator for ½ hour.

FILLING

2 pears, peeled and sliced	2 tbsp. raw sugar
2 Rome apples, peeled and sliced	1 tsp. cinnamon
¼ c. raisins	1 tbsp. butter
¼ c. nuts, chopped	1 tsp. lime juice
½ c. coconut, grated	

In bowl, combine pears and apples. Sprinkle lime juice over them. Mix in raisins, nuts, ¼ c. coconut, and 1 tbsp. raw sugar. Spoon mixture onto crust.

Preheat oven to 350°.

Sprinkle remaining coconut, raw sugar, and 1 tsp. cinnamon over top. Dot with butter. Bake for ½ hour or until crust is firm.

DRIPPY HONEYED-CASHEW PUDDING

¾ c. unsalted cashew nuts	¾ c. light honey*
½ c. grated coconut, toasted	2 tbsp. cornstarch or 1 tbsp. arrowroot
1½ c. milk	¼ tsp. salt
	2 tbsp. butter

In blender or liquifier, combine nuts and milk until smooth. Dissolve cornstarch in honey, stirring so that lumps do not form.
In saucepan, blend honey and salt over low to medium flame. Add nut mixture. Stir until a pudding texture forms.
Add butter to top. Sprinkle coconut over top.

FRISKIE FRUIT ICE CREAM

¾ c. heavy cream	½ c. pineapple juice
1 large pear, peeled	1 tsp. lemon juice
2 large plums, peeled and pits removed	2 tbsp. honey

Whip cream either in blender or with a bowl and wire whisk. Grind or blend fruit until smooth. Add juices and honey to fruit. Fold in whipped cream.
Pour mixture into baking pan. Place in freezer for 2 hrs. or until solidified.

---

* *Important:* If the honey you use is too strongly flavored, it will instantly overshadow the subtle cashew taste. This is so groovy, that it is wise to use a light honey that will not do so.

FRUIT FREEZE

1 peach, peeled, pitted and minced	¼ c. orange juice
1 orange, peeled, seeded and minced	¼ c. lemon juice
1 c. strawberries, minced	½ c. molasses
1 pear, seeded and minced	3 tbsp. brown sugar
½ cantaloupe or honeydew melon, seeded, peeled and minced	1 tbsp. cornstarch or ½ tbsp. arrowroot
	¼ c. warm water

In saucepan, combine juices, molasses, and sugar over low flame, stirring.

Dissolve cornstarch in water. Add to juice mixture. Continue stirring until a syrup forms.

In bowl, combine fruits. Pour syrup over fruits. Place in freezer compartment for at least 1 hr.

THE FURTHER ADVENTURES OF JEWISH SOUL FOOD

¾ c. white rice	1½ c. water
1 c. raisins	2 tbsp. butter
½ c. pine nuts, or almonds, blanched and cut in half	Melted butter for baking dish
1½ c. milk	1½ tsp. cinnamon
1½ tsp. cornstarch or ¾ tsp. arrowroot	3 tbsp. maple syrup
	1½ tsp. vanilla extract

In saucepan, boil water and cook rice, covered, until done. In frying pan, sauté raisins and nuts in butter for about 7 mins. Make sure to keep flame very low as they can easily burn.

Brush baking dish with melted butter. Combine all ingredients in baking dish. Preheat oven to 325°. Bake for 1½ hrs. or until milk is absorbed. This is very rich and makes 4 small portions. Increase as you like.

ITALIAN-TYPE MUNCHIES

3 c. unbleached white flour	1 c. maple syrup ½ tsp. salt Oil for deep-frying

In bowl, mix flour, syrup, and salt. Knead dough until it is pliable and soft.

On board or tabletop, roll out dough thin with rolling pin. Form a number of lumps of dough.

With your hands, roll each lump into a rope approximately 10″ long. Cut ropes at ¼″ intervals.

In frying pan, heat about 1 or 2″ of oil until crackling.

Drop in 10 pieces of dough at a time, and brown on all sides. It cooks quickly, so do not allow it to burn. Remove from oil and drain.

VARIATION

If you are really into sweets, try the following:

1 c. blanched, chopped almonds	½ c. honey ½ c. sugar

In saucepan, blend honey and sugar over medium flame. Drop drained munchies into this mixture. Remove. Roll in chopped nuts.

OATIE ENERGY COOKIES

4 c. uncooked rolled
oats
3 c. unbleached white
flour
2 c. dates, pitted and
chopped
6 tbsp. milk

1 c. brown sugar
1½ c. corn or peanut
oil
½ c. maple syrup
Oil for cookie sheets

In large bowl, beat together sugar and oil.
Add oats, syrup, flour, and milk. Mix in dates.
Preheat oven to 350°.
Oil cookie sheets. Roll dough into small balls, and flatten them on cookie sheets. Bake for 15 to 20 mins. Let cool. (Makes about 60 cookies.)

ORANGE-BANANA-VANILLA CREAM

4 med. bananas, peeled
and mashed
1 c. heavy cream,
whipped*

½ c. orange juice
¼ tsp. vanilla extract
¼ c. maple syrup
¼ tsp. cinnamon

In bowl, blend all ingredients except whipped cream, stirring. Fold in cream. Place in freezer compartment for at least 1 hr.

* When whipping cream, for best, quickest results, use a wire whip and a deep bowl.

OSCAR'S PEAR DILEMMA

4 pears, cut in half lengthwise	3 tbsp. maple syrup
¼ c. pine nuts, chopped well	¼ tsp. almond extract
½ c. almonds, blanched and chopped well	Melted butter for baking dish
	1 c. honey

Scoop out center of pears.
In bowl, combine nuts, syrup, and almond extract.
Spoon mixture into pears.
Preheat oven to 350°.
Arrange pears in buttered baking dish. Pour honey over pears.
Bake for ½ hr. or until pears are soft. Baste pears with honey once or twice.

PEANUT BUTTER PUDDING

½ c. peanut butter (smooth or crunchy)	1 c. apple juice
2 c. carrots, sliced	Oil for baking dish
½ c. raisins	
1½ c. graham crackers, crumbled	
¾ c. almonds, blanched and chopped	

In saucepan, cook carrots until soft. Drain. Mash.
Preheat oven to 350°.
In bowl, mix carrots, peanut butter, raisins, nuts,
apple juice, and 1 c. crumbs.
Spoon into oiled baking dish. Top with remaining
crumbs. Bake for ½ hr. or until crumbs are brown.

SOFT SOUR CREAM COOKIES

⅔ c. sour cream
1 c. pecans, chopped
2½ c. unbleached white
flour

⅔ c. honey
A little less than ½
c. corn or peanut
oil
½ c. maple syrup
1 tsp. nutmeg
1 tsp. cinnamon
Oil for cookie sheet

In bowl, combine honey, sour cream, pecans, oil, syrup,
nutmeg, and cinnamon.
Stir in flour, a little at a time, to form a semi-stiff
batter.
Preheat oven to 400°.
Drop batter onto oiled cookie sheets by the tea-
spoonful. Bake for 10 mins. (Makes about 34 cookies.)
Note: Cookies will be soft, rather than firm.

SOYBEAN NUTS

2 c. dry soybeans	Butter for frying
	Salt to taste

In bowl, soak beans overnight in enough water to cover. Pour off any water. In frying pan, fry in butter until brown on both sides. Add salt. Eat like nuts.

SYRUPY SWEET APPLESAUCE CAKE

1½ c. unbleached white flour	1½ c. plus 1 tbsp. brown sugar
1½ c. apple sauce*	1 c. butter
2 med. Rome apples, peeled, sliced and sprinkled with lemon juice to prevent turning brown	¼ c. maple syrup
	¼ tsp. nutmeg
	½ tsp. cinnamon
	Oil for baking pan

In bowl, cream 1½ c. sugar and butter until smooth. Mix in flour, syrup, and applesauce. Stir until smooth.
Preheat oven to 400°.
Oil baking pan. Pour batter into pan.
Arrange apple slices on top of batter. Sprinkle nutmeg, cinnamon, and 1 tbsp. brown sugar over apples.
Bake for 1 hr. or until you can pierce cake with a toothpick and have it come out clean and un-battered.

---

* If your apple sauce is homemade, rather than pre-sweetened store-bought, add a little honey or brown sugar to sweeten it.

WALNUT COOKIES

¼ c. whole wheat flour
¾ c. walnuts, chopped

¾ c. corn or peanut
oil
½ c. honey
1 tsp. anise seed
Oil for cookie sheet

In bowl, mix flour and oil. Add honey, anise seed, and walnuts. An oily dough will be formed.

Preheat oven to 400°.

Shape into balls and flatten on oiled cookie sheet. Bake for 10 to 15 mins. (Makes about 24 cookies.)

Part Two

Recipes from the Macrobiotic Diet

by Barbara Thralls

Introduction

The Macrobiotic way of eating is a wholesome diet and offers many good recipes for the cooking of grains, vegetables, and other foods. It is, however, rather restrictive in its exclusion of certain vegetarian foods, and rather permissive in its use of fish and fertilized eggs.

For those who are seriously interested in the Macrobiotic way of eating, may I suggest that you pursue the subject in greater depth in books wholly devoted to this philosophy. The recipes given here are for hungry vegetarians who enjoy nutritious and delicious meals.

General Dietary Principles Many a wise man has said, "The greatest sin we can commit is to overeat." Or as Swami Sivananda so neatly put it, "We dig our graves with our teeth." Instead of digging our graves, why not chew our way into Heaven? Chewing food thoroughly starts the digestive process by turning solid food into liquid and mixing it with the saliva. This gives the entire digestive system less work. An additional benefit is that if one chews his food thoroughly, it becomes virtually impossible to overeat. In essence, we should "drink our solids and eat our liquids."

You are what you eat. This means literally that

your physical body is composed of the food that you eat. From this standpoint, it is easy to see the importance of eating good quality foods.

What exactly is meant by "good quality foods"? Foods that are fresh and natural. This means avoiding packaged, pre-cooked, frozen, canned, chemicalized, or otherwise adulterated foods.

It is important to use fresh vegetables and fruits, preferably those in season. Your diet should vary with the seasons, in order to be in harmony with your environment. Nature shows us this by providing us with different foods at different times of the year. Is it not natural that we should eat them in this way?

Staples

GRAINS

Short-grain brown rice

Buckwheat groats (kasha)

Millet

Bulgur (wheat)

Couscous

Cornmeal (white and yellow)

Noodles (wholewheat and buckwheat)

Whole wheat flour

Whole wheat pastry flour

Brown-rice flour

Buckwheat flour

Unbleached white pastry flour

BEANS

Aduki beans   Chick-peas

(Black beans, Pinto beans, Red kidney beans, Lentils, etc.)

SEAWEED

Hiziki   Nori

Wakame   Kombu

DRIED FRUIT AND NUTS

Raisins   Almonds (raw)

Walnuts (raw)   Cashews (raw)

BEVERAGES

Bancha tea	Pero coffee
Mu tea	Kokkoh

MISCELLANEOUS

Sea salt	Cold-pressed corn oil
Cinnamon	Cold-pressed sesame oil
Tahini (sesame paste)	Kuzu starch (used medicinally)
Tamari (soy sauce)	Arrowroot starch
Miso soybean paste	Apple butter

Where and How to Buy   You can purchase all these products in any health-food store, and many of them in your supermarket. As far as quantity is concerned, it is a good idea to have a stock of your staples.

Grains—keep at least 2 lbs. of every grain. You will probably need about 5 to 10 lbs. of whole wheat flour.

Beans—2 lbs. of each type of bean is adequate, with the exception of Aduki beans. These beans are so high in protein, and so delicious, that you will probably want to stock about 5 lbs. of them.

Seaweed, Beverages and Miscellaneous—With all these articles it is best to start off with one package of each, and experiment with them.

Dried Fruit and Nuts—2 lbs. of each is an adequate beginning.

The vegetables and fruits you buy should always be fresh. If you are able to obtain them, organic vegetables are preferable; if not, you should always make sure to scrub your vegetables well.

Tools

Storage Containers   All grains, and most other staples, should be stored in airtight containers, not in paper bags. It seems trivial, but this will keep your grains fresh and insect free.

Pots and Pans
1. Cast-iron skillet #8 or #10 for sautéeing and general use. It provides even distribution of heat and its thickness prevents burning.
2. Stainless steel or heavy-bottomed soup pot—6 quart
3. Small stainless steel saucepan—1½ or 2 quart
4. Pressure cooker—4 or 6 quart. An excellent utensil for cooking grains and vegetables to retain their vitamins and minerals.
5. Casserole dish
6. Lids for all pots and pans
7. Bread pans—2 or 3 loaf pans, 5″ x 8″ in size
8. Cookie sheet
9. 8″ or 9″ pie plate
10. 2″-deep oven pan
11. 3″-deep pot for deep frying

Other Cooking Utensils   Most of the following items can be purchased in large department stores, health-food stores, or in Chinese or Japanese sections of large cities.

1. Nituke (vegetable) knife—a flat, well-balanced knife, absolutely essential for cutting vegetables and fruits (but NEVER cut anything else with it, as that will dull and nick the blade permanently).

2. Wooden implements should always be used for handling food, such as rice paddles, spoons, and cooking chopsticks, for stirring and serving.

3. Asbestos pads—2 or 3 to place under pots while cooking to prevent burning.

4. Vegetable scrubbing brush to remove dirt and sprays.

5. Oil brush

6. Grater

7. Apple corer

8. Food mill or blender

9. Whip

10. Suribachi (mortar and pestle)

11. Oil skimmer for deep-frying.

Recipes

❦ GRAINS

Grains are a good, substantial food, giving long-lasting and high-quality energy. They are exceptionally desirable in winter, although the Macrobiotic diet includes them year round. All leftover grains should be kept out of the refrigerator (chilling or freezing food kills the life energy). Leftovers can be used in a multitude of ways. See "Vegetable-grain Combinations" on page 120, "Suggestions for Leftovers" on page 149, or use your own imagination.

*All grains contain Vitamin B_2, B_6, D, calcium, phosphorus, magnesium, iron, protein, fat, and natural sugars. Wheat is especially rich in Vitamin A and B_1. Buckwheat (kasha) has large quantities of B_2, E, magnesium, calcium, and amino acids. Oats are rich in fat, as is corn. Oats also contain the most mineral salt, with barley second. Those grains richest in protein are buckwheat (enormous amount), whole wheat, and oats.**

The main staple of the Macrobiotic diet is short-grain brown rice. Considered the perfectly balanced food, it should be pressure-cooked for best results. And always remember the importance of chewing very well!

* (See Abehsera, Michel, *Zen Macrobiotic Cooking*, University Books, Inc., New York, N.Y., 1968, pp. 15–20.)

BOILED BROWN RICE

1 c. brown rice   **Water for washing rice**
                             ¼ tsp. sea salt
                             2 c. cold water

Wash rice three times as for Pressure-cooked Brown Rice (see below).

Place all ingredients in pot. Bring to boil, lower flame and simmer for 1 hr. until the liquid is evaporated and there are holes in the rice. The bottom of the pot should be slightly scorched. Let sit for 10 minutes. Mix well before serving. Serves 2 or 3.

PRESSURE-COOKED BROWN RICE

1 c. brown rice   **Water for washing rice**
                             ¼ tsp. sea salt
                             1½ c. cold water

Wash rice three times by adding cold water to the pot, swishing around with your hands and emptying water out through strainer.

Combine all ingredients in cooker, place asbestos pad underneath and turn flame up full. When pressure comes up (15 lbs.), lower flame to simmer, and cook for 45 mins. Remove from flame and allow pressure to return to normal. Let sit for 10 mins. before serving. Serves 2 or 3.

RICE CREAM

1 c. rice cream	½ tsp. corn oil
	4 c. cold water
	¼ tsp. sea salt

In pan, sauté rice cream in oil over fairly high flame, stirring constantly with a firm, steady stroke until there is a nutlike fragrance. Remove from pan and cool.

Place in pot, slowly add water, stirring constantly to remove lumps. Add salt.

Bring to boil, lower flame, simmer for 30 to 40 mins. until creamy.

You may add either Tamari or raisins to taste.

BULGUR WHEAT

1 c. bulgur wheat	1 tsp. corn oil
	3 c. boiling water
	¼ tsp. sea salt
	Tamari soy sauce

In saucepan, heat oil over medium-high flame. Sauté bulgur, stirring constantly, until it turns darker and has a nutlike fragrance.

Add water and salt. Lower flame, cover, and simmer for 10 to 15 mins. until all water is gone.

Add Tamari to taste. Serves 3.

CORNMEAL

1 c. cornmeal

2 tsp. corn oil
3½ c. boiling water
¼ tsp. sea salt
Tamari soy sauce

In pan, heat oil over medium-high flame. Sauté cornmeal well, stirring constantly until it darkens and has a nutlike fragrance, about 5 to 10 min. (Be sure to sauté it long enough. If cornmeal is not properly sautéed, it retains its bitterness and is not very tasty. If done correctly, it will be very sweet.) Remove from pan and let cool.

In pot, boil water. Add the cornmeal and salt to the water by sifting to prevent lumping and, with the other hand, stir constantly.

Lower flame, cover and cook for 30 to 45 mins.

Add Tamari to taste.

Cornmeal makes an excellent dinner served with Miso Soup (please see p. 130) and Vegetable Tempura (please see p. 114).

COUSCOUS

1 c. couscous

¼ tsp. salt
2 c. boiling water
Tamari soy sauce

In saucepan, add couscous and salt to boiling water. Turn off flame and cover. Let stand for 10 mins.

Add Tamari to taste. Serves 3.

Couscous is a very light grain, delicious combined with sautéed vegetables (please see p. 112). Leftover couscous added to bread dough makes a very sweet and soft loaf.

FLAKES

2 c. assorted flakes	2 tsp. corn oil
(rice, rye, wheat,	4 c. boiling water
barley, millet, etc.)	½ tsp. sea salt
	Tamari soy sauce

In saucepan, heat oil over medium-high flame. Sauté flakes, stirring constantly, until they turn dark and have a nutlike fragrance.

Add water and salt, cover and simmer for 20 to 25 mins., stirring occasionally.

Add Tamari to taste.

Flakes are delicious with sautéed parsnips (please see p. 113).

KASHA (Buckwheat Groats)

1 c. groats	1 tsp. corn oil
	2 c. boiling water
	¼ tsp. sea salt
	Tamari soy sauce

In pot, sauté groats in oil over fairly high flame until they darken and have a nutlike fragrance (about 3 to 5 mins.).

Add water (be careful, it sputters), and turn down flame. Add salt, cover, and simmer for about 10 mins.

Add Tamari to taste, once it is done.

Kasha is delicious with any vegetable sauce, or mixed with rice. Another way to serve it (for those who are not Macrobiotic) is with sour cream.

KASHA CROQUETTES

1 c. buckwheat groats	4 c. water
(kasha)	2 tsp. corn oil
¼ c. scallions, sliced	¼ tsp. sea salt
in rounds	Tamari soy sauce
1 c. whole wheat flour	Corn oil for deep frying

In saucepan, boil water.

In a deep, 2″ frying pan, heat 1 tsp. oil over medium-high flame. Add groats and sauté, stirring constantly until it has a nutlike fragrance (about 5 mins.) Add boiling water and salt. Cover, lower flame, and simmer for 15 mins. Let cool.

In small frying pan, heat 1 tsp. oil, add scallions, and sauté over medium-high flame for a few mins. until they become green and soft. Remove from flame and let cool.

Season kasha with Tamari to taste. Add flour and mix well. Add cooled scallions and mix.

Knead to firm consistency. Form into balls or egg shapes and roll in dry flour.

Heat 3″ of corn oil in a deep saucepan over a medium-high flame (too high causes smoking). When oil begins to move, and sputters if water is dropped into it, it is ready.

With chopsticks or tongs, gently place 3 or 4 balls in oil at a time. They will cook quickly. Remove when they have turned dark and hard on the outside. Drain on paper towels. Makes 16 balls (3 or 4 per person).

These croquettes are delicious served with Scallion Wheat Sauce (please see p. 133).

Note: These croquettes may also be pan-fried in a small amount of oil or baked for 40 mins. at 300°.

MILLET

1 c. millet	1 tsp. corn oil
	4 c. boiling water (in pressure cooker, use 3 c.)
	¼ tsp. sea salt
	Tamari soy sauce

In pot or pressure cooker, heat oil over medium-high flame. Sauté the millet, stirring constantly until it turns dark and has a nutlike fragrance.

Add boiling water and salt. Cover, lower flame, and let simmer for 30 mins. (in pot or pressure cooker).

Add Tamari to taste.

Millet is a heavy winter grain, delicious with Miso Soup (please see p. 130) on a cold day.

NOODLES (*Buckwheat or Whole Wheat*)

In choosing noodles, there are two excellent brands from which to pick. Hime Brand makes a nice, light noodle. Chico San is heavier but also of good quality. Try both and see which you prefer.

1 package noodles	1 tsp. sea salt
	3 qts. boiling water
	3 c. cold water plus cold water for rinsing

ιn pot, add noodles to salted, boiling water. When water returns to a boil, add 1 c. cold water.

Repeat this twice more and test noodles. If they are not yet soft, leave on flame until soft. Remove from flame and let sit for 10 mins., covered. Drain* and rinse with cold water to prevent sticking.

To serve hot, pour boiling water over noodles.

Serve with any vegetable sauce or with soup poured over noodles.

There are several noodle recipes in the Vegetable-Grain section (please see pp. 120–124).

* Noodle water is excellent when added to bread doughs. It improves the taste and, most important, makes the bread rise higher.

🌺 VEGETABLES

PRESSURE-COOKED VEGETABLES

Any vegetables may be pressure-cooked. They are very gentle and easily digested when cooked this way. Carrots are especially delicious when pressure-cooked.

Cut the vegetables in large chunks, place in cooker with enough water to cover the bottom of the pot and prevent burning.

Sprinkle a little salt over the top, mix it around, and put the lid on the cooker. Place on high heat. Once the pressure comes up (15 lbs.), lower the flame and simmer. Here are the cooking times and water measurements for some standard vegetables:

	Minutes	Water Cup(s)
Asparagus	2½	½
Beans (wax or string)	3	½
Lima Beans	2	½
Broccoli	2½	½
Brussels Sprouts (whole)	5	¾
Cabbage (sliced)	3	¾
Cabbage (whole)	8	¾
Carrots (sliced)	2½	¼
Carrots (small, whole)	4	¼
Cauliflower	3	½
Celery	5	½
Corn on the Cob	5	1
Corn Kernels	3	½
Kale	4–6	½
Kohlrabi	6	½
Onions (sliced)	3	½
Onions (medium whole)	7–10	¾
Parsnip (sliced)	2	½
Parsnip (halved)	7	¾
Peas	2	½
Pumpkin (pieces)	5–10	1¼
Rutabagas	5	¾
Spinach	1½	½
Squash	5	¾
Squash (Hubbard)	8–10	¾
Turnips (sliced)	5	¾

Once the vegetables have been cooked for the specified time, turn off flame, remove pot from stove, and allow pressure to return to normal. Serve immediately. The water is most delicious to drink, or put in a bread dough.

SAUTÉED VEGETABLES

Sautéeing is a most tasty and healthy way to cook vegetables. By coating the vegetable with hot oil, the vitamins and minerals are "locked in" and not lost in cooking, as may happen with other methods.

It is good to combine 2 to 4 types of vegetables when sautéeing, although there is no rule to prevent the use of just one at a time. Any combination will do, but it is important to consider color and texture also. A nice variety of each is pleasant; for instance, onion, cabbage, cauliflower, and carrots.

INGREDIENTS

2 medium-sized onions	Corn oil for sautéeing
½ medium-sized cabbage	Pinch sea salt
½ cauliflower	Tamari soy sauce (optional)
4 medium-sized carrots	

Scrub the vegetables well with a vegetable brush. In order for the vegetables to sauté quickly, they must be cut properly, always thin, and never "helter-skelter." There is a definite method to cutting vegetables.

Onions   Cut each onion in half, through the core, and then stand it up and cut in pie-shaped pieces. The result will be slivers attached to the core.

Cabbage   Cut the whole cabbage in half through the core. Turn it down on its flat side, and cut in strips from top to bottom. Detach the core from the central pieces, and cut it in thin slices separately.

Cauliflower   Break into flowerettes and slice into thin pieces.

Carrots   Slice thin pieces, cutting diagonally, to expose a greater amount of surface area.

Keep each vegetable in a separate bowl.

In frying pan, place a small amount of corn oil (enough to cover pan bottom).

Heat over a medium-high flame.

Sauté one vegetable at a time, starting with the light-colored vegetables and going to darker ones. Each vegetable will undergo a change when fully sautéed.

Do not add the next vegetable until you see that change (*i.e.,* onions become soft and translucent, cabbage becomes greener and soft, cauliflower becomes semi-transparent and soft, etc.).

Add each new vegetable by clearing a space for it so that it will immediately come into contact with the hot oil, and then cover with the hot vegetables.

After all the vegetables have been sautéed, lower the flame, cover, and let the vegetables cook in their own juices for 25 to 30 mins., stirring occasionally.

Right before serving, add a pinch of salt and, if desired, a dash of Tamari.

NITUKE VEGETABLES

Prepare the same way as Sautéed Vegetables (please see preceding recipe), but when it is time to lower the flame and cover the pan, add a small amount of water to the bottom of pan. Let the vegetables cook for 30 mins. longer in the steam, stirring occasionally and adding more water if necessary.

TEMPURA (BATTER-FRIED VEGETABLES)

THE BATTER

There are many different combinations of flours to be used in making Tempura batter. I have found that it is always tasty if one half of the proportioned flour is corn flour. Sweet-rice flour gives an interesting flavor. You may use it instead of brown-rice flour. Unbleached white flour makes the batter light and crisp, and can be substituted for the pastry flour. Experiment, using your own imagination.

INGREDIENTS

½ **cup corn flour**	½ **tsp. sea salt**
¼ **cup brown-rice flour**	**1 to 1¼ cups cold**
¼ **cup whole wheat**	**water**
pastry flour	**Oil for deep frying**

In bowl, mix the dry ingredients together.

Add the water and mix. The batter should be quite loose.

Refrigerate.

THE VEGETABLES

Just about any vegetable (or fruit) is delicious cooked this way. (Try apples or peaches!) Some good vegetables are:

Carrots, cut diagonally as for sautéeing.

Onions, cut in rings, or keep each section attached to the core.

Watercress—stalks

String beans—cut off ends, keep whole

Cauliflower—flowerettes
Broccoli—flowerettes
Squash—small pieces

You may use any vegetable you choose. However, cabbage and lettuce should be avoided due to their excessive water content.

Wash and cut vegetables and refrigerate. In a deep saucepan, heat 3" of oil over a medium-high flame (high heat causes smoking). When the oil begins to move rapidly (5 to 10 mins.), test it with a drop of water. If the oil sputters, it is ready.

Remove vegetables from refrigerator. Dip each vegetable in the batter, swish it around, and with chopsticks or tongs carefully place it in oil. Put in 3 or 4 pieces at a time. (If you put in any more, the oil will lose its heat.) The vegetables should cook very quickly. If not, the oil is not hot enough. After 2 or 3 mins. they should be golden and crisp.

Remove from oil and drain on paper towels. Eat immediately as vegetables become soggy very quickly.

Any extra batter may be dropped into oil by the spoonful and cooked separately.

SAUCE

This is to be placed on the table in bowls and each piece of tempura should be dipped into it as you eat.

1 tsp. ginger,
    grated (approx.)
6 tsp. Tamari soy sauce
3 tsp. cold water

In each bowl, combine above ingredients, adjusting measurements to your liking. Serve one bowl to each person.

BAKED ACORN SQUASH

1 large acorn squash	Pinch sea salt and/or Tamari soy sauce
	Corn oil for brushing

Cut squash in half and remove seeds. Sprinkle sea salt and/or Tamari over it, *lightly.* Brush all exposed areas of squash with corn oil. Place in oven pan and bake in preheated oven at 350° to 375° for 50 to 60 mins. until soft.

This is a heavy vegetable dish, delicious in winter. You may stuff the squash with the following mixture.

STUFFING

1 large onion, chopped fine	3 tsp. corn oil
¼ head of cabbage, chopped fine	½ c. cold water
1 small carrot, sliced in thin rounds	Pinch sea salt
⅓ c. unbleached white flour	

In small saucepan, heat 1 tsp. oil over medium-high flame. Add the flour and sauté until it darkens and has a nutlike fragrance. Remove from flame and cool.

In a frying pan, heat the remaining oil over medium-high flame and sauté the vegetables, adding one at a time—the onion, cabbage, and lastly the carrot.

Once all have been sautéed, lower flame, cover, and simmer for 10 mins. in vegetables' own juices.

In bowl, add water and salt to the flour and mix. The consistency should be fairly loose. More water may be added if necessary. Combine this mixture with the vegetables, fill the squash, and oil the edges of squash. Place in oven pan and bake at 400° for 45 to 50 mins.

CHINESE VEGETABLES

4 scallions, sliced in rounds
1 Chinese cabbage (celery cabbage), sliced in rounds
6 stalks celery, sliced diagonally (see Sautéed Vegetables —carrots)
½ c. white radishes, sliced in rounds
1 red pepper, diced (optional)
1 green pepper, diced (optional)
8 mushrooms, diced (optional)
1 handful bean sprouts (optional)

Corn oil for sautéeing
3 c. cold water
Water for diluting arrowroot
3 tbsp. arrowroot starch
Pinch sea salt
Tamari soy sauce

In frying pan, place a small amount of oil—enough to cover bottom. Heat over medium-high flame.

Sauté one vegetable at a time, beginning with light-colored ones and ending with darkest one (please see instructions for Sautéed Vegetables p. 112).

After all vegetables have been added and are soft, add the 3 c. water and bring to a boil. Lower the flame, cover, and simmer for 20 mins.

In a bowl, dilute arrowroot with small amount of water. Add to vegetables, stirring constantly until you have a thick and translucent sauce.

Add salt and Tamari to taste and let cook a few mins. longer.

Serve over rice. Serves 4 to 5.

BOILED CARROTS AND SPINACH IN SAUCE

4 med. carrots, whole	**Water for boiling**
1 bunch spinach, whole	

In pot, boil carrots for 20 mins. In separate pot, boil spinach for 5 mins. Cool both to lukewarm and cut in 1″ pieces.

Pour Scallion Tahini-Tamari Sauce (please see p. 132) over it and serve.

SQUASH PIE

CRUST

1 c. whole wheat flour	**¼ tsp. sea salt**
or whole wheat	**¼ c. corn oil**
pastry flour	**½ to ¾ c. cold water**

In bowl, mix flour and salt. Add oil and rub between hands until the oil is spread evenly throughout and the mixture is crumbly. Add the water a little at a time to form the dough (the less water, the crisper the crust). Knead to proper consistency. Form into a ball and let sit for ½ hr.

FILLING

3 large or 4 med. onions, diced	2 tsp. corn oil
1 large butternut squash, sliced thin	Water for pressure cooker
	1 tsp. sea salt
	Tamari soy sauce

In sauce or frying pan, heat oil over medium-high flame. Add onions and sauté, stirring constantly, until transparent. Add squash and sauté until it gets quite mushy.

Transfer vegetables to pressure cooker, add a small amount of water to bottom to prevent sticking, and then add salt. Pressure-cook for 20 mins. or boil until tender.

Strain through food mill or blend in blender. Add Tamari to taste (if necessary) and set aside.

TOPPING

Handful of millet

Heat a dry cast-iron pan over a high flame. Add millet. Roast, stirring constantly, until millet becomes dark and gives off a nutlike fragrance. Set aside (you may prepare a larger quantity and store it.)

On a lightly floured board, roll out the pie dough. Place in an 8″ or 9″ oiled pie plate and flute edges with a fork. Puncture bottom in a few places with fork. If you wish, you may bake the shell by itself for 10 mins. at 400°.

Add the filling, sprinkle the top with millet, and bake in preheated 450° oven until crust and top of pie are slightly browned—about 15 to 25 mins.

VEGETABLE-GRAIN COMBINATIONS

FLAKES LOAF

4 c. assorted flakes
1 to 2 c. cooked vegetables
1 tsp. corn oil
6 c. boiling water
1 tsp. sea salt
Tamari soy sauce

In saucepan, sauté flakes in oil over a medium-high flame until they darken and have a nutlike fragrance. Add boiling water and salt, lower flame, and cook uncovered for 15 to 20 mins. until flakes have a loose cereal consistency. Season with Tamari to taste.

Mix in vegetables and then place mixture in an oiled casserole dish. Pat top down with wet rice paddle.

Bake in preheated 400° oven for 50 to 60 mins. until top is crisp and golden. Serves 6.

Any vegetable sauce can be served with this. Parsnip sauce is especially delicious.

FRIED RICE (OR NOODLES)

2 sheets Nori
1 umeboshi plum
4 scallions, sliced in
    rounds
2 c. cooked rice (or
    noodles)

3 tsp. corn or sesame oil
Tamari soy sauce

Toast Nori by passing each sheet over a high flame on the stove until it becomes crisp and can be easily crumbled. Crush into small pieces and set aside.

Break plum into small pieces. Throw away pit.

In frying pan, heat oil over medium-high flame. Add scallions and sauté until transparent (2 to 3 mins.).

Add rice (or noodles), Nori, and umeboshi, stirring well, as the mixture sticks easily. Keep stirring until all is coated with oil, and hot. Add Tamari to taste.

LEFTOVER CASSEROLE

4 c. leftover noodles
    (or other grain)
3 to 4 c. sautéed vege-
    tables
2 c. vegetable sauce or
    thick soup (squash
    or other)

Oil for casserole dish

In bowl, mix ingredients well.

Place in oiled casserole dish. Pat the top down with a wet rice paddle.

Bake in preheated 300° oven for 30 mins. or until top is golden and crusted. Serves 6 to 8.

PIROSHKI (VEGETABLE OR GRAIN-FILLED TURNOVERS)

TURNOVER

1 c. whole wheat flour	½ tsp. sea salt
1 c. whole wheat pastry flour	½ c. corn oil
	½ to ¾ c. cold water

In bowl, mix dry ingredients. Add oil. Rub between the hands until the oil is evenly distributed and the mixture is crumbly.

Slowly add ½ to ¾ c. water to form dough. Knead to workable consistency. Let sit for ½ hr.

FILLING

Small amount of left-over grain or vegetables, or a combination of both	Oil for pan and for brushing

Divide dough into 4 pieces. On board or tabletop roll out fairly thin into 5" circles.

Place small amount of filling inside dough circle. Fold up and flute edges with fork. Wet the edges, if necessary.

Place in oiled oven pan, and brush top side of turnovers with oil. Bake in preheated 350° oven for 20 mins. These also may be pan-fried in a small amount of oil or deep-fried.

RICE AND VEGETABLE PIE

CRUST

(for two 9″ crusts)

1 c. whole wheat flour	½ tsp. sea salt
1 c. whole wheat pastry	½ c. corn oil
flour	½ to ¾ c. cold water

In bowl, mix dry ingredients. Add oil. Rub well between hands until oil is evenly distributed throughout and flour is crumbly.

Add water slowly to form dough. Knead to proper consistency, about the consistency of your ear lobe. Let sit for ½ hr.

FILLING

2 c. brown rice, cooked	Corn oil for pie plate
1 c. vegetables, cooked	and brushing
1 c. of any vegetable sauce (please see p. 134.	

In bowl, mix rice and vegetables. Add sauce. Mix well. Correct the seasoning, if necessary.

On board or tabletop, roll out dough after separating into two balls—one slightly larger than the other.

Grease an 8″ or 9″ pie plate and place the larger circle in it. Flute the edges with fork.

Fill with rice mixture. Add top circle and seal two crusts together by fluting with fork. Puncture top crust with fork in a few places. Brush the top with oil.

Bake in 450° oven for 20 mins. or until top is golden brown and crisp. Serves 6.

"VEGG ROLLS"
(VEGETARIAN EGG ROLLS)

ROLL

1 c. whole wheat flour	½ tsp. sea salt
1 c. whole wheat pastry flour	¼ c. corn oil
	½ to ¾ c. cold water

In bowl, mix dry ingredients. Add oil. Rub between the hands until oil is evenly distributed and mixture is crumbly.

Slowly add the water to form dough. Knead to the proper consistency, about the consistency of your ear lobe. Let sit for ½ hr.

FILLING

3 large cabbage leaves	Water for boiling
Small amount cooked vegetables or grains (about ¼ c.)	Pinch sea salt

In pot, boil cabbage leaves in salted water until they become slightly limp and can be easily rolled.

On board or tabletop, roll out the dough in 6 pieces, each about 3″ square, not too thin.

Cut the cooled cabbage leaves in half and place a small amount of vegetable or grain inside each one and roll it.

Place each cabbage roll inside a square of dough on the diagonal. Fold over the corners, wetting the dough slightly, if necessary, to make it stick to itself.

In pan, deep-fry, or bake in preheated 350° oven for 30 mins., or until crust is crisp and golden. Makes 6 individual rolls.

🌸 BEANS

ADUKI BEANS, BLACK BEANS OR CHICK-PEAS

Aduki beans are an excellent source of protein and also have healing effects upon the kidneys and other organs. All three types of beans are cooked in the same way. Black beans and chick-peas should be soaked several hours before cooking.

PRESSURE-COOKED

½ c. beans

Water for washing beans
1¼ c. cold water
⅛ tsp. sea salt
1 to 1⅓ tsp. Tamari soy sauce

Wash the beans in the pressure cooker three times by adding twice as much water as you have beans, swishing beans and water around with your hand to loosen the dirt, and pouring the dirty water out. (You will be amazed at the amount of dirt these beans can sometimes collect.) After the third washing, empty all the water out.

Add 1¼ c. cold water to beans in pressure cooker. Do *NOT* add salt, as this will keep the beans from becoming tender.

Cover and cook over high heat until the pressure comes up. Reduce heat and simmer for 45 mins.

Take off flame. Let pressure return to normal. Remove cover, add salt and Tamari.

If there is a great deal of excess liquid, cook slowly, uncovered, until most of liquid is absorbed. The remainder will thicken when cooled. Serves 3.

BOILED

½ c. beans   **Water for washing beans**
                              2 c. cold water
                              ⅛ tsp. sea salt
                              1 to 1½ tsp. Tamari soy sauce

Wash as above. Put beans and 2 c. of water in pot.

Bring to boil, lower flame, and simmer over a tiny flame for about 2 hrs.

Remove cover, add salt and Tamari, and cook uncovered until liquids boil off. It will thicken when cooled. Serves 3.

ADUKI MUFFINS

1 c. Aduki beans,   **½ tsp. salt**
  cooked and seasoned   **2½ c. cold water**
2 c. whole wheat flour   **Oil for muffin tin**

In bowl, mash beans and set aside.

In another bowl, mix flour and salt. Add water—forming a very loose mixture—mixing well.

Oil muffin tin and fill each slot half full of batter. Add a layer of beans and fill remainder of each cup with batter. Bake 45 mins. at 350°. Makes 12 muffins.

These muffins can be stuffed with various ingredients—such as apple butter or applesauce, nuts, raisins, chestnut purée, etc. Use your own imagination.

🌺 SEAWEED

HIZIKI

1 c. dried hiziki	Water to cover hiziki
	2 tsp. corn oil
	½ tsp. sea salt
	2 to 4 tsp. Tamari soy sauce

In bowl, soak hiziki in water for 20 to 30 mins., until it has expanded fully. Squeeze out water and save it for cooking.

In frying pan or pot, heat oil over medium-high flame. Add hiziki (be careful, it may sputter) and sauté for 2 mins., stirring constantly.

Add the water from soaking and bring to a boil. Lower flame and simmer for 30 mins. If water boils off, add a little more. Cook for another 20 mins., until there is only a small amount of liquid left.

Add salt and Tamari and cook for 5 mins.

Hiziki is excellent mixed with rice. And also, it makes your hair shiny!

HIZIKI AND CARROTS
(or *LOTUS ROOT*)

¾ c. carrots or lotus root, scrubbed and sliced diagonally	Water to cover hiziki
	3 tsp. corn oil
	½ tsp. sea salt
	2 to 4 tsp. Tamari
1 c. dried hiziki	soy sauce

If you are using the dried lotus root, you must let it soak overnight. In bowl, soak hiziki in water for 20 to 30 mins. while washing and cutting vegetables.

When hiziki has expanded fully, squeeze out the water and save it for cooking.

In frying pan or pot, heat oil over medium-high flame. Add carrot or lotus root and sauté, stirring constantly, until vegetable softens and changes color.

Add hiziki and sauté for 2 mins., stirring constantly. Continue as for hiziki (preceding recipe).

NORI

Toast sheets of Nori, one at a time, by passing them over a high flame until each sheet becomes crisp and can be easily crumbled. Crush it into small pieces, or cut it.

Nori is good as a seasoning, either on the table or in cooking. It may also be used to roll rice balls in, and served as a pretty party treat.

WAKAME

| 2 c. wakame, loosely packed | Water to cover wakame
2 tsp. corn oil
½ tsp. sea salt
2 to 4 tsp. Tamari
soy sauce |

Cook as for Hiziki (please see p. 127).

 SOUPS

BARLEY BEAN SOUP

| 1 c. beans (pintos or red kidneys are best, but any kind will do)
2 c. vegetable parts*
1 c. barley | Water for washing beans
8 c. cold water
½ to 1 tsp. sea salt
Tamari soy sauce |

Wash beans. In pot, soak beans and vegetable parts overnight in the water.

Add barley and bring to a boil. Lower flame, cover and simmer for at least 2 hrs., adding more water as needed to keep it at the same level. (The longer, the better—red kidney beans really don't even begin to taste good until after 4 hrs. of cooking!) Remove the vegetable parts. Add salt and Tamari to taste. Serves 6.

* That is, carrot tops, cauliflower cores, broccoli stems, cabbage leaves, etc.

MISO SOUP

2 c. onions, slivered	12 c. water
4 c. cabbage, sliced	1 tbsp. corn oil
2 c. carrots, sliced	6 heaping tbsp. Miso
diagonally	soybean paste

Wash and cut the vegetables (please see Sautéed Vegetables, p. 112, for cutting instructions).

In frying pan, heat oil over medium-high flame. Sauté the vegetables in oil, beginning with the onions, then adding cabbage, then carrots, one at a time. Stir constantly. (Please see directions for sautéeing, p. 112).

In pot, put water up to boil. When all vegetables are thoroughly sautéed, add them to boiling water.

Let soup return to a boil. Lower flame and cook, uncovered, for 30 to 60 mins. (the longer, the better).

About 10 mins. before the end, dilute Miso in bowl in a small amount of the soup. Mash Miso until it becomes creamy. Add to soup, mix well, and let it cook into soup.

Taste after 10 mins. and adjust seasoning if necessary. Serves 10 to 12.

Miso is an excellent source of protein. It gives great strength and warmth. A delicious wintertime dish.

SQUASH SOUP

1 bunch scallions, sliced	1 tbsp. corn oil
diagonally	8 c. cold water
1 large butternut	½ tsp. sea salt
squash, sliced thin	Tamari soy sauce

Wash and cut vegetables.

In soup pot, heat the oil over medium-high flame. When oil is hot, add scallions and sauté until green and soft. Add squash and sauté until just mushy, stirring constantly.

Add water and bring to a boil. Simmer until squash is soft—about 15–20 mins. Mash squash or blend in blender.

Add salt and Tamari to taste. Serve immediately. This soup is a quickie and loses flavor when cooked for a long time. Serves 8.

TAMARI-NOODLE SOUP

2 c. onions, sliced	12 c. water
4 c. cabbage, sliced	1 tbsp. corn oil
2 c. carrots, sliced diagonally	2 tsp. sea salt
1 package whole wheat noodles	½ to 1 c. Tamari soy sauce

Wash and cut vegetables.

In frying pan, heat the oil over medium-high flame. Beginning with the onions, sauté vegetables one at a time, stirring constantly.

In pot, put water on to boil.

When all vegetables are thoroughly sautéed, add them to the pot. Let soup return to boil. Lower flame and cook covered for 30 to 60 mins. (the longer, the better).

About 10 mins. before the end, add salt and Tamari. Let this cook into soup for the remaining 10 mins. Taste and adjust seasoning, if necessary.

You may either cook the noodles directly in the

soup by adding them to the boiling liquid about 10 mins. before the end and cooking them until soft; or, by boiling them separately in salted water, as per instructions on p. 109. If you cook them separately, pour cold water over them to prevent sticking. Then when soup is ready, arrange noodles in each bowl and pour soup over them. You may also add a sprig of parsley or some crushed-up Nori to float on top of the soup. Serves 10 to 12.

This soup tastes much like broth or bouillon and is a nice, soothing treat on a cold winter's day.

 SAUCES

SCALLION-TAHINI-TAMARI SAUCE

1 bunch scallions	**1 to 1½ tsp. corn oil**
1 tbsp. Tahini	**1½ c. cold water**
	3 tbsp. Tamari soy sauce

Wash scallions and chop fine.

In saucepan, heat oil over medium-high flame.

When hot, add scallions and sauté, stirring constantly, until they become green and soft.

Add water, cover, and bring to a boil. Lower flame and simmer for 20 mins.

In bowl, mix Tahini and Tamari well. Add mixture to saucepan. Mix well. Cover and simmer for 5 mins. longer.

Adjust seasoning to taste.

This sauce should be poured over cooked grains or boiled or pressure-cooked vegetables. It is best with boiled carrots and spinach (please see p. 118).

SCALLION-WHEAT SAUCE

6 scallions, sliced diagonally	4 tbsp. corn oil
	1 c. cold water
4 tbsp. unbleached white or whole wheat pastry flour	½ tsp. sea salt
	4 tsp. Tamari soy sauce

In saucepan, heat oil over medium-high flame. When hot, add scallions and sauté, stirring constantly, until they become green and soft. Blend in flour. Remove from flame and cool.

Once cool, add water, stirring constantly. Bring to a boil, lower flame, and simmer for 10 to 20 mins. Add more water, if necessary.

Add salt and cook 5 mins. Add Tamari and cook a few mins. longer. Serves 6.

This sauce is delicious over any grain, especially Kasha Croquettes (please see p. 108).

STANDARD VEGETABLE SAUCE

½ c. brown-rice flour
or whole wheat
flour
1 large cauliflower,
sliced thin

3 tsp. corn oil
4 c. cold water
Small amt. of water
for flour paste
2–3 tsp. Tamari soy
sauce
¼ tsp. sea salt

Heat a dry frying pan. Add flour and toast over medium-high flame, stirring constantly.

When flour gives off a nutlike fragrance and is just beginning to brown, remove from flame, transfer to a bowl and let cool.

In frying pan, heat oil over medium-high flame. Add cauliflower and sauté, stirring constantly, until it becomes transparent and soft.

When fully sautéed, add water and bring to a boil. Lower flame, cover, and simmer for 20 to 30 mins.

While this is cooking, add small amount of water to flour to make a thin paste. When cauliflower is finished cooking, stir in this paste until mixture becomes thick and creamy (1 to 2 mins.).

Add salt and Tamari, mix well, and let cook a few mins. longer.

This sauce may be made with parsnips, Brussels sprouts, or any other vegetable that has a fairly strong flavor. Try this sauce over flakes (please see p. 107) or kasha (p. 107).

🌸 SPREADS

PARSLEY, PEA, ZUCCHINI SPREAD

1 c. peas	1 tsp. corn oil
1 c. zucchini, diced	½ c. cold water
3 tbsp. Miso	Small amt. of water for
6 tbsp. Tahini	dissolving Miso
	1 c. fresh parsley,
	chopped fine

Wash and cut vegetables, as per above.

In frying pan, heat oil over medium-high flame. Add parsley and sauté until it turns greener and becomes limp, stirring constantly. Add peas and zucchini, one at a time.

When all vegetables have been thoroughly sautéed, add water. Bring to boil, lower flame, and cover. Simmer for 20 mins.

In bowl, dissolve Miso with small amt. of water by mashing with a fork until it becomes a thick and creamy paste. Set aside.

Add Tahini to vegetables and mix in well. Cook on a low flame for 10 to 15 mins.

Add Miso and stir well. Let cook a few mins. longer. Serve hot or cold.

This spread can be made with any vegetables you choose. The best kind are those which become soft and fall apart easily when cooked.

TAHINI-MISO SPREAD

12 tbsp. Tahini   **4 tbsp. Miso soybean
                                    paste
                                    Small amt. of water
                                    to dissolve Miso**

In bowl, dissolve Miso with water by mashing with a fork until mixture is thick and creamy. Set aside.

Heat a dry frying pan over medium-high flame. Add Tahini. Continue to cook, stirring constantly, until Tahini becomes darker and gives off a wonderful nut-like fragrance (about 10 to 15 mins.).

Add creamed Miso to Tahini and stir well, blending them together. Remove from flame. Serve either hot or cold, on bread.

🪷 BREADS

OVERNIGHT GRAIN BREAD

**3 c. whole wheat flour   ¾ tsp. salt
3 c. cooked grains   1 to 2 c. cold water or
Flour for kneading   Bancha Tea
                             Oil for bread pan and
                               brushing**

In bowl, add salt to flour and cooked grains. Mix well.

Gradually add liquid, stirring constantly. Mix well and knead on floured board.

When dough is one even consistency, place in bowl and cover with damp cloth. Place in warm spot and let sit for 10 to 14 hrs. until dough just begins to smell. (If you let it sit too long, bread will have a sour taste.) Place in oiled bread pan. Brush top with oil. Bake in a preheated 350° oven for 1½ hrs. or until crust is dark and fairly hard.

If you have done all this correctly, the bread will rise nicely.

OVERNIGHT WHOLE WHEAT BREAD

4 c. whole wheat flour　　**1 tsp. sea salt**
Flour for kneading　　　　**2 to 3 c. cold water**
　　　　　　　　　　　　　or Bancha Tea
　　　　　　　　　　　　　Corn oil for bread pan
　　　　　　　　　　　　　and brushing

In bowl, add salt to flour. Gradually add liquid, stirring. Mix well. Knead on floured board.

When dough is one even consistency (it should be quite dry), place in a bowl and cover with a damp cloth. Place bowl in a warm spot and let sit for 10 to 14 hrs. until the dough just begins to smell. (If you let it sit too long, bread will have a sour taste.)

Place dough in oiled bread pan. Brush top with oil. Bake in a preheated 350° oven for 1½ hrs. or until crust is dark and fairly hard.

If you have done all this correctly, the bread will rise nicely.

SESAME CRACKERS

1 c. whole wheat flour
2 tbsp. roasted sesame
  seeds

¼ tsp. sea salt
1 to 1¼ c. cold water
Oil for cookie sheet

In bowl, mix dry ingredients. Gradually add water, stirring constantly. Mix well. The batter should be fairly loose but slightly lumpy.

Drop batter by tablespoonsful onto an oiled cookie sheet. Bake in a preheated 350° oven for 30 mins. (Makes 12 crackers.)

🌸 DESSERTS

APPLE BUTTER

10 to 15 apples, washed,
  cored, and sliced
  in crescents

Small amt. of water
  for cooking (about
  1 to 2 c.)
Pinch sea salt
Pinch cinnamon

Place apples in pressure cooker or pot with enough water in bottom to prevent burning. Add salt and cinnamon, stirring in well. Cover and bring to pressure (or boil). Lower flame and cook for 5 mins. at full pressure, or boil until apples break up and become mushy.

Let pressure come down.

Strain apples through food mill. Place strained apples in heavy-bottomed pot. Bring to boil. Lower flame and simmer, uncovered, until dark and thick (3 to 4 hrs.).

Cool and serve with bread or toast.

APPLE CRISP

4 to 6 apples, peeled, cored, and sliced in crescents
2 c. whole wheat pastry flour
1 c. rolled oats

Pinch of cinnamon
Pinch of sea salt
½ c. corn oil
1 c. apple juice

Line the bottom of a 2"-deep baking pan (8" x 8") with apple slices.

In bowl, mix cinnamon with juice and pour *half* the mixture over apples.

In another bowl, mix flour, oats, and salt. Add oil and stir until mixture is crumbly. Add remaining juice and mix. (The mixture should still be crumbly.) Sprinkle mixture over apples and let sit for ½ hr.

Bake in a preheated oven at 400° until apples are soft and top is beginning to brown. Serves 8 to 10.

APPLE PIE WITH KUZU FROSTING

CRUST

1 c. whole wheat pastry flour	¼ tsp. salt Pinch of cinnamon ¼ c. corn oil ¼ to ½ c. cold apple juice

In bowl, mix dry ingredients. Add oil and rub well between the hands until oil is evenly distributed throughout and flour is crumbly.

Add apple juice slowly to form dough. Knead to proper consistency, about the consistency of your ear lobe. (The less you knead it, the better.) Let sit for ½ hr.

FROSTING

1 to 1½ c. cold apple
juice
1 tbsp. kuzu or arrow-
root starch
Small amt. of water
to dissolve kuzu

In saucepan, heat apple juice over small flame. Dissolve kuzu in water until it forms a thick liquid.

Add kuzu to juice and let cook, uncovered, stirring regularly until it becomes thick and clear. Let cool.

FILLING

2 or 3 cooking apples, peeled, cored, and sliced in rounds	Pinch of cinnamon Pinch of sea salt

Roll out pie crust. Line a 9″ pie plate with crust and flute edges with a fork. Make a few punctures on bottom of crust with fork to prevent shrinkage. Arrange apple slices in pie shell. Sprinkle lightly with cinnamon and salt. Bake in preheated 375° oven for 35 to 45 mins. or until apples begin to turn brown. Remove from oven. Pour kuzu mixture over top and let cool.

APPLE SAUCE

10 to 15 apples, washed, cored, and sliced in crescents	Small amt. (about 1 to 2 c.) of water for cooking Pinch sea salt Pinch cinnamon

Place apples in pressure cooker or pot with water in bottom to prevent burning. Add salt and cinnamon, stirring in well.

Cover and bring to pressure (or boil). Lower flame and cook for 5 mins. at full pressure, or boil until apples break up and become mushy.

Let pressure or boil come down. Cool and serve.

FRUIT TEMPURA
(Batter-Fried Fruit)

BATTER

½ c. corn flour
½ c. whole wheat
pastry flour

Pinch sea salt
Pinch cinnamon
½ c. cold water or
apple juice

In bowl, mix dry ingredients. Add liquid gradually, stirring as you add. The batter should be quite loose. Refrigerate.

This batter will be enough for 3 to 4 apples.

FRUIT

Apples or peaches seem
to work best, but
use your own
favorites

Corn oil

Wash fruit and cut into crescent shapes. In a deep saucepan, heat 2 or 3″ of oil over a medium-high flame (too high heat causes smoking). When oil begins to move rapidly (about 5 to 10 mins.), test it with a drop of water. If water sputters, oil is ready. Dip each piece of fruit in batter and then put this mixture into oil, placing each piece in as gently as possible. It will cook very quickly. Cook no more than 3 or 4 pieces at a time as more than that will reduce the heat of the oil. Remove each piece when golden brown. Drain on paper towels. Estimate ½ apple or peach per person.

And be careful not to burn your mouth while eating as the fruit retains the heat for quite awhile!

RUGGELAH *(Rolled Pastry)*

2 c. whole wheat pastry flour	¼ tsp. sea salt
3 handfuls raisins	¼ tsp. cinnamon
3 handfuls chopped walnuts	¼ c. corn oil
Apple butter	¼ to ½ c. ice cold water or apple juice

In bowl, mix flour, salt, and cinnamon. Add oil and rub well between the hands until it is evenly distributed throughout and the flour is crumbly.

Add the liquid slowly to form dough. Knead to the proper consistency. Let sit for ½ hr.

Wash raisins and chop nuts into bite-size pieces. Roll out dough in a circle to ¼″ thickness.

Spread apple butter lightly over the entire circle, leaving a ½″-wide unbuttered edge. Sprinkle raisins and nuts generously over dough. Roll dough, moistening it if necessary to make it stick to itself.

When completely rolled up, seal the edge and ends by fluting with a fork.

Cut into 2″ pieces and bake in 375° oven for 30 to 40 mins. or until crust is golden.

Makes six individual pieces.

SAUTÉED FRUIT CHAUSSONS

DOUGH

2 c. whole wheat pastry flour	½ c. corn oil
	½ to ¾ c. cold water or apple juice
	½ tsp. sea salt
	½ tsp. cinnamon

In bowl, mix dry ingredients. Add oil and run mixture between the hands until oil is evenly distributed throughout.

Add liquid slowly to form dough. Knead to proper consistency, about the consistency of your ear lobe (the less you knead it, the better). Let sit for ½ hr.

FILLING

6 apples, peeled, cored, and sliced in thin crescents

1 to 2 handfuls raisins, washed

1 handful walnuts, chopped in tiny pieces

1 tbsp. corn oil

Pinch sea salt

Pinch cinnamon

In frying pan, heat oil over medium-high flame. Add apples and sauté them, stirring constantly. They take a fairly long time to become soft, approx. 10 to 15 mins.

As soon as apples become pulpy, add the rest of the ingredients. Cook for just a few mins., lowering the flame to simmer. Remove from heat.

Roll out the dough into circles ½" thick and 3" in diameter.

Place a small amount of the apple mixture on one half of each circle.

Fold the circle in half, and seal by fluting the edges with a fork.

Bake in preheated 350° oven for 30 mins. (You may use any filling you choose in these pastries—use your own ingenuity!)

🏵 SEASONINGS FOR THE TABLE

GOMASIO

Sesame seeds

Water for washing seeds
Sea salt

You may make a large amount and store it in a sealed container. It stays fresh for about a week. The proportion should always be 10:1—sesame seeds:salt.

Wash sesame seeds 3 times in water and drain.

Heat a dry frying pan over medium-high flame. Add seeds and roast, stirring constantly, for about 15 mins. until they give off a nutlike fragrance and will crush easily when rubbed with the fingers. If they can't be crushed, they are not ready and will not have a nice flavor. When finished, remove from flame and place in bowl.

In a dry frying pan, over high flame, heat the salt. Cook for 5 mins., stirring constantly, until it crystallizes.

Remove from pan. Measure the 10:1 ratio of seeds to salt into either a suribachi or mortar and pestle. Grind until 80% is powder.

Place in sealed container. Use on the table instead of salt.

🌷 BEVERAGES

BANCHA TEA (*Herb Tea*)

You may roast a large amount of leaves and store them for a long time.

4 c. tea leaves

Heat a dry frying pan over high flame. Add leaves and roast for about 5 mins., stirring constantly, until brown (*not black*).

Remove from pan immediately. Store in a jar.

For 1 cup of tea, heat 1 c. of water to boiling. Add a pinch of roasted leaves. Simmer for 10 mins. Strain and serve.

For a pick-me-up on a cold day, add 1 tsp. Tamari. It creates a flavor similar to chicken broth.

MU TEA

1 package Mu Tea   2 qts. water

In saucepan, add tea to water. Boil for 10 to 20 mins. Serves 6.

This is a medicinal drink containing 16 herbs. It can be bought in packets at any health-food store. It can be served cold in summer and the grounds can be used twice.

KOKKOH

2 heaping tbsp. kokkoh   3 c. water

In saucepan, add kokkoh to water. Boil for 10 mins., stirring constantly to prevent burning. Serves 2.

This is a milk substitute, good if you are feeling weak.

PERO COFFEE

1 tsp. pero   1 c. water

In saucepan, heat water to boiling. Put pero in cup. Add water and stir.

This is an instant cereal beverage. It is an excellent substitute for coffee and actually tastes much better.

UMEBOSHI DRINK

1 salted umeboshi plum   1 qt. water

In saucepan, add plum to water and bring to a boil. Lower flame and simmer for 1 hr.

Strain and serve. Serves 2.

In summertime, this can be served cold. It relieves thirst.

🪷 SUGGESTIONS FOR LEFTOVERS

There are many recipes in the Vegetable-Grain Section which call for cooked grains or vegetables, seaweed, etc. Other uses are as follows.

1. Any leftover grain may be added to a soup as a thickening.
2. Any leftover grain may be used to make the overnight grain bread (please see p. 136). Especially sweet and tasty are millet, kasha, or couscous.
3. Leftover rice can be
   a. compressed into balls and deep-fried
   b. compressed into balls, wrapped in sheets of toasted nori, and served cold as an appetizer.
   c. mixed with apple juice, raisins, nuts, and Tahini, cooked on a low flame for 20 to 30 minutes, allowed to cool, and served as rice pudding.
4. Leftover kasha can be used in Kasha Croquettes (please see p. 108), or in the Leftover Casserole (please see p. 121).
5. Leftover noodles (or rice) can be
   a. added to soup
   b. fried with vegetables (please see p. 121).
6. Leftover vegetables can be added to soups or breads.
7. Extra seaweed can be added to soups, also.
8. Beans can be used in vegetable pies or muffins (please see pp. 123 and 126), or as filling for Piroshki (please see p. 122).

🌸 SIMPLE RECIPES

The following recipes require short cooking time:

Index

vegetarian cooking,
11–12
Topping, squash pie,
119–120
Turnovers, vegetable or
grain-filled, 122
Tzimmes, 83

Umeboshi drink, 147
Upma, 63
Utensils, *see* Tools

Vegetable-cheese dish, 75
Vegetable-filled turn-
overs, 122
Vegetable-grain   combi-
nations,   120–124
egg rolls, 124
flakes loaf, 120
leftover casserole, 121
pie, rice and vegetable,
123
piroshki, 122
rice, fried, 121
Vegetable roast, 76–77
Vegetables
artichoke hearts, fried,
81–82
batter-fried, 114–116
beans, 13, 125–126
barley   bean   soup,
129
boiled, 126
Florentine, 81
pressure-cooked,
125–126
broccoli
gingered, 82–83
smoky, 71
cabbage, cauliflower

and, Kashmirian,
70
stuffed, 73
carrots
hiziki and, 128
spinach and, boiled,
in sauce, 118
cauliflower, cabbage
and, Kashmirian,
70
chick-peas
boiled, 126
pressure-cooked,
125–126
Chinese, 117–118
eggplant
baked, Merf and
Mildred, 65
curry, 67–68
diced, 67
parmigiana, 68
lentil
loaf, 52–53
soup, Indian, 33
Macao noodles and, 56
macaroni and, 57
mushrooms, stuffed,
74–75
nituke, 113
pea, parsley, zucchini
spread, 135
peppers, soybean-
tomato mix,
stuffed, 71–72
potato curry, 70–71
potato-fruit casserole,
69
pressure-cooked, 110–
111
rice and, pie, 123

SWS
6/72